Learn to Speak and Write SPANISH

Published by :
Lotus Press Publishers & Distributors

Learn to Speak and Write SPANISH

Sudhir Khanna

Lotus PRESS

4735/22, Prakash Deep Building
Ansari Road, Darya Ganj,
New Delhi - 110002

Lotus Press : Publishers & Distributors
Unit No. 220, 2nd Floor, 4735/22, Prakash Deep Building,
Ansari Road, Darya Ganj, New Delhi- 110002
Ph.: 41325510, 98118-38000
• E-mail : lotuspress1984@gmail.com
www.lotuspress.co.in

Learn to Speak and Write Spanish

ISBN: 81-89093-88-6

Printed & Published by : **Lotus Press Publisher & Distributors,** New Delhi-02

Introduction To The Book...

Our books on **FOREIGN LANGUAGES** have been designed keeping in mind the increasing number of tourists, businessmen and others who visit these countries very often.

These books can also serve as a basis for a complete study of these languages.

Learners who use these books can easily make themselves understood where these languages are spoken. By reading these books, one is not required to learn a long list of grammatical rules.

The vocabularies in these books have been carefully selected to give every learner the words that are needed in all aspects of everyday life.

We, at Lotus Press, are pretty confident that these books will give the learners a useful introduction to these languages as they are spoken and written. This can eventually lead the learners to achieve a complete mastery on their chosen language.

LEARN TO SPEAK AND WRITE **SPANISH** helps you to get acquainted with the Spanish language. This will surely enable you to speak and write Spanish as fluently just the way the typical Spaniards do. Happy learning ...

– Publishers ◆

◆ TABLE OF CONTENTS ◆

Lesson 1

The Spanish Alphabet

Alphabet	Pronunciation
A	ah
B	bay
C	say
CH	chay
D	day
E	ay
F	ayfay
G	khay
H	ahchay
I	ee
J	khoatah
K	kah
L	aylay
LL	ayyay
M	aymay
N	aynay

Ñ	aynyay
O	oa
P	pay
Q	koo
R	ayray
S	aysay
T	tay
U	oo
V	bay
W	bay doablay
X	aykees
Y	eegryaygah
Z	Saytah

Lesson 2

Pronunciation: Vowels and Consonants

English speakers generally find the pronunciation of Spanish vowels easy. Close approximations of all their sounds exist in English and, with the exception of the *E* and the sometimes-silent *U*, all the vowels have basically one sound.

The main thing to keep in mind is that in Spanish the vowels' sounds are generally more distinct than they are in English. In English, any vowel can be represented by what's known as the schwa, an unstressed vowel sound such as the 'a' in 'about', the 'ai' in 'mountain', and the 'u' in 'pablum'. However, in Spanish, such an indistinct sound isn't used. Although, as in most languages, the sounds of the vowels can vary slightly with the letters before and after them, in general the sound remains the same regardless of the word it's in.

A

It is pronounced similarly to the 'a' in 'father' or the 'o' in 'loft'. Examples: *madre, ambos, mapa.* There are some speakers who sometimes pronounce the *a* something halfway between the 'a' in 'father' and the 'a' in 'mat', but in most areas the first sound given is standard.

I

It is pronounced similar to the 'ee' in 'feet' and the 'e' in 'me', although usually a little briefer. Examples: *finca, timbre, mi.*

O

It is pronounced like the 'oa' in 'boat' or the 'o' in 'bone', although usually a little briefer. Examples: *teléfono, amo, foco.*

Now, the two vowels whose sound can change:

E

It is generally pronounced like the 'e' in 'met' when it is at the beginning or within a word. It is pronounced similarly to the Canadian 'eh', kind of a shortened version of the 'é' in the English 'café', when it is at the end of the word. Sometimes it can be somewhere between those two sounds. It's not quite the sound of the English letter 'A', which if pronounced slowly often has an 'ee' sound at the end, but closer to the 'e' of 'met'. Keep in mind that even when it's at the end of the word, in a sentence it may sound more like the 'e' of met. For example, in a phrase such as *de vez en cuando*, each *e* has approximately the same sound. Examples: *café, compadre, embarcar, enero.*

U

It is generally pronounced like the 'oo' in 'boot' or the 'u' in 'tune'. Do not pronounce it like the 'u' in 'uniform'. Examples: *universo, reunión, unido.* In the combinations *gui* and *gue*, as well as after *q*, the *u* is silent. Examples: *guía, guerra, quizás.* If the *u* should be pronounced between a *g* and *i* or *e*, an umlaut *(sometimes called a diaeresis)* is placed over it. Examples: *vergüenza, lingüista.*

Diphthongs and triphthongs

As in English, two or three vowels in Spanish can blend together to form a sound. The sound is basically the sound of the two or three vowels rapidly pronounced. For example, the *u* when followed by an *a, e, i* or *o* ends up sounding something like the 'w' in 'water'. Examples: *cuaderno, cuerpo, cuota.* The *ai* combination sounds something like the sound of 'eye'. Examples: *hay, airear.* The *i* when followed by an *a, e, i* or *u* sounds kind of like the 'y' in 'yellow'.: *hierba, bien, siete.* And other combinations are possible as well: *miau, Uruguay, caudillo.*

Y

Generally, the *y* is pronounced the same as it would if it were an *i*, as part of a diphthong. Examples: *rey, soy, yacer.* In some words that are derived from English and have a *y* at the end often retain the English pronunciation. For example, in popular songs you may hear words such as *sexy* and phrases such as *oh baby.*

Pronunciation: Easy Consonants

One factor that makes Spanish pronunciation fairly easy for English speakers is that many of the consonants are pronounced almost like their English equivalents. Although there are some subtle differences in a few cases, generally you can pronounce the consonants covered in this chapter as you would in English and be easily understood–provided you're doing OK on your other letters, of course !

One thing to keep in mind about Spanish consonants is that they're generally softer and somewhat less distinct than their English equivalents *(the most notable exceptions are the r and rr)*. Although their vowel sounds may be distinct, some *hispanohablantes* may sound to the untrained ear like they're mumbling. Keep in mind that there are some regional variations as well, although if you follow the descriptions in these Chapters you will be understood.

Here are the pronunciations of the consonants with sounds most like English's:

C

It at least in most of Latin America, is pronounced like the 'c' in 'cereal' when it comes before an *e* or an *i* and like the 'c' in 'car' when it is in other positions. Examples: *complacer, hacer, ácido, carro, acabar, crimen.* **Note:** Although you will be understood if you use the Latin American pronunciation, in parts of Spain the *c* sounds like the 'th' in 'thin' when it comes before an *e* or *i.*

CH

It is pronounced the same as the 'ch' in 'church'. Examples: *chico, machismo, Chile.*

F

It is pronounced like the 'f' in 'fox'. Examples: *eficaz, frío, frenesi.*

K

It has basically the same sound in Spanish, although

somewhat softer. It is found primarily in words of foreign origin. Examples: *kilómetro, Irak.*

M

It is pronounced like the 'm' in 'mother'. Examples: *madre, música, embajada.*

P

It is pronounced like the 'p' in 'spot'. Note that the 'p' in 'spot' is softer and less explosive than the 'p' in 'pot'. Examples: *papas, padre, suponer.*

Q

It is pronounced the same as the *k*. Note that the *u* following a *q* is not pronounced. Examples: *quetzal, psiquiatra, que.*

S

It is pronounced like the 's' in 'simple'. You do not give it the 'z' sound heard in 'wears' and many other English plural words, although it can be slightly voiced (like a soft 'z') when it comes before an *m, b, d, v, g, l, n* or *r*. Examples: *Susana, seres humanos, sencillo, fantasma.*

T

It is pronounced like the 't' in 'stop'. Note that the 't' of 'stop' is softer and less explosive than the 't' of 'top'. Examples: *todo, yate, temer.*

W

It is pronounced like the 'w' in 'water'. It is found primarily in words of foreign origin. Examples: *whisky, Zimbabwe.*

Y

It is generally pronounced the same as in English.

Examples : yacer, yate.

Pronunciation: Difficult Consonants

While many of the Spanish consonants have sounds that are similar to those in English, many are distinctly different.

B and V

These are pronounced exactly the same. In fact, one of the few spelling problems that many Spanish speakers have is with these two letters, because they don't distinguish them at all from their sound. Generally, the *b* and *v* are pronounced like the 'b' in 'beach'. When either of the letters is between two vowels, the sound is formed kind of like the English 'v', except that the sound is made by touching the lips together instead of the upper teeth and lower lip. Examples: *bebé, ambos, vencer.*

D

It generally is pronounced somewhat like the 'd' in 'diet', although often the tongue touches the bottom of the teeth instead of the top. But when d comes between vowels, it has a much softer sound, kind of like the 'th' in 'that'. Examples: *derecho, helado, diablo.*

G

It is pronounced much like the English 'g' in 'go', except when it precedes an *i* or *e*. In those cases, it is pronounced like the Spanish *j*. Examples: *gordo, gritar, gigante, mágico.*

H

It is always silent. Examples: *hermano, hacer, deshacer.*

J

It can be difficult, as its sound that of the German *ch*, is absent in English except for a few foreign words where it is sometimes retained, as in the final sound of ***(loch)*** or the initial sound of *Channukah.* The sound is sometimes described as a heavily aspirated 'h', made by expelling air between the back of the tongue and the soft palate. If you can't pronounce it well, you'll be understood by using the 'h' sound of 'house', but it's worthwhile to work on the correct pronunciation. Examples: *garaje, juego, jardín.*

L

It is always pronounced like the first 'l' in 'little', never like the second one. Examples: *los, helado, pastel.*

LL

It is usually pronounced like the 'y' in 'yellow'. There are some regional variations, however. In parts of Spain it has the sound of the 'll' in 'million', and in parts of Argentina it has the 'zh' sound of 'azure'. Examples: *llama, calle, Hermosillo.*

N

Usually has the sound of the 'n' in 'nice'. If it is followed by a *b, v, f* or *p*, it has the sound of 'm' in 'empathy'. Examples: *no, en, en vez de,* and*ar.*

Ñ

It is pronounced like the 'ny' in 'canyon'. Examples: *ñoño, cañón, campaña.*

R and RR

These are formed by a flap of the tongue against the roof of the mouth.

Example : radio, zorro

X

It varies in sound, depending on the origin of the word. It is often pronounced like the 'x' in 'example' or 'exit'.

Z

It generally sounds like the 's' in 'simple'. In Spain it is often pronounced like the 'th' in 'thin'. Examples: *zorro, vez*.

Stress and Accent Marks

Knowing how letters are pronounced is only one aspect of learning Spanish pronunciation. Another key aspect is knowing which syllable should be stressed.

Fortunately, in Spanish the rules for stress (also known as accent) are straightforward. In fact, there are only three basic rules that cover nearly every word:

.If a word ends in a vowel, *n* or *s*, the stress is on the penultimate (next to last) syllable. For example, ***to**ro*, *computa**do**ra*, ***jo**ven* and *za**pa**tos* all have their accent on the next-to-last syllable. Most words fit this category.

Words that end in other letters have the stress on the last syllable. For example, *ho**tel***, *ha**blar***, *encendedor* and *vir**tud*** all have the accent on the final syllable.

If a word isn't pronounced according to the above two rules, an accent is placed over the vowel of the syllable that gets the stress. For example, *co**mún***, ***lá**piz*, ***mé**dico*, *in**glés*** and *oja**lá*** all have the stress on the indicated syllable.

The only exceptions to the above words are some words of foreign origin, generally words adopted from English that retain their original spelling and pronunciation. For example, *sandwich* is usually spelled without an accent over the initial *a*, even though the stress is as in English. Similarly, personal names and place names of foreign origin usually are written without accents (unless accents are used in the originating language).

You should be aware that sometimes accent marks are used only to distinguish two similar words and they don't affect pronunciation (because the marks are already on a syllable that is being stressed). For example, *el* and *él* are both pronounced the same way, even though they have quite different meanings. Similarly, some words, such as *que* and *quien*, use accent marks when they appear in questions, but usually not otherwise. Accents that don't affect pronunciation are known as orthographic accents.

Lesson 3

Articles

Definite Articles

The word 'the' occupies a unique place in the English language as the only word that grammarians classify as a definite article. It's not quite so simple in Spanish, where the English 'the' has four equivalents. Like many adjectives, the definite article in Spanish varies with number and gender:

	Singular	Plural
Masculine	***el***	***los***
Feminine	***la***	***las***

Although there are a few exceptions, as a general rule a definite article is used in Spanish whenever 'the' is used in English. But Spanish also uses a definite article in many cases where English does not. Although the following list isn't exhaustive and there are exceptions to some of these rules, here are the major instances where Spanish includes a definite article absent in English:

With abstract nouns and nouns used in a general sense: In English, the article is often omitted with abstract nouns and nouns that refer more to a concept than a tangible item. But it still is needed in Spanish. A few examples might help clarify: *La ciencia es importante. (Science is important.) Creo en la justicia. (I believe in justice.) Estudio la literatura. (I study literature.) La primavera es bella. (Spring is beautiful.)*

With most titles of people: The definite article is used before most titles of a person being talked about. ***El** presidente Bush vive en la Casa Blanca. (President Bush lives in the White House.) Voy a la oficina de **la** doctora González. (I'm going to the office of Dr. Gonzalez.) Mi vecina es **la** señora Jones. (My neighbour is Mrs. Jones.)* The article is omitted, however, when directly addressing the person. *¿Cómo está usted? profesora Barrera. (How are you, Professor Barrera?)*

Before days of the week: Days of the week are always masculine. Except in constructions where the day of the week follows a form of *ser (a verb for 'to be')*, as in *hoy es martes (today is Tuesday)*, the article is needed. *Vamos a la escuela **los** lunes. (We go to school on Mondays.) El tren sale **el** miércoles. (The train leaves on Wednesday.)*

Before verbs used as subjects

In Spanish, infinitives *(the basic form of a verb)* can be used as nouns. The article *el* is used when one is used as the subject of a sentence. ***El** escribir es difícil. (Writing is difficult.) **El** esquiar es peligroso. (Skiing is dangerous.) No me gusta **el** nadar. (I don't like swimming. In Spanish, this sentence has an inverted word order that makes nadar the subject.)*

Often before names of languages

The article generally is used before names of languages. But it can be omitted when immediately following a verb that is used often with languages, such as *hablar* (*to speak*) or after the preposition *en*. ***El** inglés es la lengua de Belice.* (*English is the language of Belize.*) ***El** alemán es difícil.* (German is difficult.) *Hablo bien **el** español.* (*I speak Spanish well.*) But, *hablo español.* (*I speak Spanish.*) *No puede escribir en francés.* (He can't write in French.)

With some place names

Although the definite article is seldom mandatory with place names, it is often used with many of them. The list of place names using the definite article is quite arbitrary and can be found here. ***La** Habana es bonita. (Havana is pretty.)* ***La** India tiene muchas lenguas. (India has many languages.)*

With nouns joined by 'and'

In English, it often isn't necessary to include the 'the' before each noun in a series. But Spanish often requires it. *La madre y **el** padre están felices. (The mother and father are happy.) Compré la silla y **la** mesa. (I bought the chair and table.)*

Singular Indefinite Articles: Un and Una

If you listen to popular music, you may recall one of the sentences of a Spanish-language dance tune: *Yo no soy marinero, soy capitán, soy capitán.* Translated that would be, 'I am not a mariner, I am a captain, I am a captain'.

That sentence indicates one of the differences between Spanish and English. Whereas as English requires the word 'a' before 'mariner' and 'captain', Spanish doesn't require an equivalent word, which in this case would be *un.*

The words 'a' and 'an' are known to grammarians as indefinite articles and the Spanish equivalents are *un (used before masculine nouns and noun phrases)* and *una (feminine).* Using the Spanish indefinite articles when they aren't needed is one of the pitfalls for many students beginning to learn Spanish . Say *no soy un marinero, soy un capitán* and it would sound as awkward *(and improper)* as one possible translation into English: 'I am not one mariner, I am one captain'.

Generally speaking, whenever you use *un* or *una* in Spanish, you need to use 'a' or 'an' to say the equivalent in English. But the reverse isn't true. The appearance is that Spanish frequently 'omits' the indefinite articles. Although the rules of article usage can get complex and there are cases where the use of *un/una* is discrctionary, here are the most common cases where the article shouldn't be used even though it's used in English:

Before an unmodified noun after a form of *ser* ('to be'), especially in reference to occupation, religion, affiliation or social status *(normally, if the noun is modified, the article should be used) Soy profesor. Él es un buen dentista. ¿Eres católica? No, soy una metodista feliz. Es artista. Es una artista que muere de hambre.* I'm a professor. He is a good dentist. Are you Catholic? No, I'm a happy Methodist. She is an artist. She is a starving artist.

Before *otro* ('other') *Quisiera otra taza. Compró otro coche.*

I would like another cup. He bought another car.

Before *mil ('thousand')* and *cien ('hundred') Gana mil*

dólares por mes. Tiene cien años. He earns a thousand dollars per month. She is a hundred years old.

In exclamations using *qué* ('*what*') *¡Qué lástima! ¡Qué casa!* What a pity! What a house!

After *con* ('with') and *sin* ('*without*') *Come con cuchara. Escribe sin ordenador.* She eats with a spoon. He writes without a computer.

Frequently after forms of *tener* ('to have'), *comprar* ('to buy'), *llevar* ('to wear') and some other verbs when generically referring to things that people would normally have or use one at a time *No tengo coche. Lleva camisa. Vamos a comprar casa. ¿Tiene madre?*

I don't have a car. He is wearing a shirt. We're going to buy a house. Does he have a mother?

If you're a beginner in Spanish, don't sweat the details of the final rule for now. As you use the language, you will get a feel of whether you need the article or not.

Finally, there is one case where we don't use the indefinite article in English where it's needed in Spanish: in a series of two or more words joined by 'and' (*y in Spanish*). In English we might say 'a cat and dog', but in Spanish it must be *un gato y un perro.* Without the second *un,* the phrase would be understood as referring to one creature, a cross between a cat and dog. Note the distinction between these sentences: *Conozco a un artista y un dentista* means 'I know an artist and I know a dentist', while *Conozco a un artista y dentista* means 'I know a dentist who is also an artist'.

Plural Indefinite Articles: Unos and Unas

Now you must be familiar with the very common Spanish words *un* and *una,* which are used before nouns and are the equivalent of 'a' or 'an' in English. These words are known as singular indefinite articles.

In Spanish, these words can also exist in the plural form; *unos* and *unas* are known as the plural indefinite articles. Although they don't have an exact English equivalent, they are usually translated as 'some' or 'a few'; if one is used before a number, it usually means 'about' or 'approximately'. Like adjectives, the article must agree with the noun in number and gender. See examples of the plural indefinite articles in these sample sentences:

Compré ***unas*** *manzanas.*

I bought **a few** apples.

Unos *alumnos salieron.*

Some students left.

Tengo ***unos*** *casetes nuevos.*

I have **some** new cassettes.

La película duró ***unos*** *noventa minutos.*

The film lasted **about** 90 minutes.

Tomamos ***unos*** *refrescos.*

We had **some** soft drinks.

Necesité ***unas*** *horas para leer el libro.*

I needed **a few** hours to read the book.

As is the case with singular indefinite articles, the plural article is needed before each of the items in a series: *Compré* ***unas*** *manzanas y* ***unas*** *peras.* I bought **some** apples and pears.

If *unos* or *unas* is used before an item that exists in the plural to refer to a single object (*as 'pants' or 'glasses' in English*), the article can mean 'one' or 'one pair of': *Necesito* ***unas*** *gafas de buceo.* I need **a pair of** diving goggles.

Lesson 4

Nouns

Noun: Gender

Just as maleness or femaleness is an inherent characteristic of human beings and most animals, so is gender an inherent characteristic of nouns in Spanish. With only a few exceptions, mostly those of occupations such as *dentista*, the gender of nouns doesn't change with the context and a noun's gender determines the form of many adjectives that describe it.

Although Spanish nouns are classified as either feminine or masculine, remember that there can be feminine nouns that describe things we think of as masculine and vice versa. For example, ***el*** *elefante* refers to an elephant whether it's male or female. For some people, it might be easier to think of them as simply two classifications rather than giving them a sexual identity. Unlike German and some other Indo-European languages, Spanish has no neuter nouns. *(There are a few neuter pronouns, such as* ***lo*** *and* ***ello****, which are used under limited circumstances, however.)*

The basic rule is that masculine nouns go with masculine adjectives and articles and feminine nouns go with feminine adjectives and articles. *(In English, the articles are 'a', 'an' and 'the'. Also note that in Spanish many adjectives don't have separate masculine and feminine forms.)* And if you use a pronoun to refer to a masculine noun, you use a masculine pronoun; feminine pronouns refer to feminine nouns.

Nouns and adjectives that end in *-o (or -os for plural)* generally are masculine and nouns and adjectives that end in *-a (or -as for plural)* generally are feminine, although there are exceptions. For example, *cada día* means 'each day'. ***Día*** ('day') is a masculine noun; ***cada*** ('each') can be either feminine or masculine.

Since you can't always tell by looking at a noun or knowing its meaning whether it's masculine or feminine, most dictionaries use notations (*f* or *m*) to indicate the gender. And it's also common in vocabulary lists, such as many of them at this site, to precede words with an ***el*** for masculine words and a ***la*** for feminine words. (*El* and *la* both mean 'the'.)

Here is a chart that shows some of the ways a noun's gender affects the usage of other words. Some of the examples may be more understandable once you study adjectives, articles and pronouns.

Masculine	**Feminine**
the man: ***el*** *hombre*	the woman: ***la*** *mujer*
a man: ***un*** *hombre*	a woman: ***una*** *mujer*
the man: ***los*** *hombres*	the women: ***las*** *mujeres*
the fat man: *el hombre* ***gordo***	the fat woman: *la mujer* ***gorda***
some men: ***unos*** *hombres*	some women: ***unas*** *mujeres*

He *(the man)* is fat: ***Él** es gordo.*

She *(the woman)* is fat: ***Ella** es gorda.*

If you have two or more nouns that are being described by a single adjective and they are of mixed genders, the masculine adjective is used.

Example

*El **carro** es **caro***, the car is expensive. *La **bicicleta** es **cara***, the bicycle is expensive. *El **carro** y la **bicicleta** son **caros***, the car and the bicycle are expensive.

Noun: Plural

In English, as you already know, we usually make nouns plural by adding '-s' to the end of the word, unless it ends in '-y', in which case the '-y' is dropped and replaced by an '-ies'. (Hyphens indicate word endings, not that a hyphen is used.) In Spanish, it is almost as simple and Spanish has few of the numerous and unpredictable exceptions that English has.

The basic rule

The rule that you follow most of the time is roughly the same as the rule in English: If a word ends in a consonant, add ***-es***. If it ends in an unaccented vowel, simply add an ***-s***. In Spanish, ***y*** is treated as a consonant for purposes of pluralising.

Examples

un árbol (one tree), dos árboles (two trees); el actor (the actors), *los actores (the actors)*; *el hotel (the hotel), los hoteles (the hotels)*; *un taco (a cue), dos tacos (two cues)*; *un perro (a dog), tres perros (three dogs); un rey (a king), cuatro reyes (four kings).*

Orthographic changes

Some words follow the general rule in terms of pronunciation, but a change in either a letter or an accent mark is needed. In plurals of words that end in **-z**, the **-z** changes to ***-ces*** for the plural. And if the addition of ***-es*** would change which syllable gets the accent, an accent is either dropped or added.

Examples

el juez (the judge), los jueces (the judges); una vez (once), dos veces (twice); el inglés (the Englishman), los ingleses (the Englishmen); la canción (the song), las canciones (the songs); el examen (the exam), los exámenes, the exams.

Words ending in stressed vowels

Words that end in a stressed ***-é*** form the plural simply by adding **-s**. Words that end in other stressed vowels have an *-es* added. There are four common exceptions: *el papá (the daddy), los papás (the daddies); una mamá (a mother), dos mamás (two mothers); el dominó (the domino), los dominós (the dominoes);* and *un sofá (a sofa), tres sofás (three sofas).*

Examples

el rubí (the ruby), los rubíes (the rubies); el hindú (the Hindu), los hindúes (the Hindus); el café (the coffee), los cafés (the coffees).

Finally, the exceptions

The above rules cover probably 99 per cent of the nouns

you will use. Most of them are words that are identical in the singular and plural–e.g., *la crisis* (*the crisis*), *las crisis* (*the crises*)–and new words of foreign origin, which often follow the pluralising rules of the originating language–e.g., *el applet Java* (the Java applet), *los applets Java* (the Java applets). As a beginner, the main exceptions you need to know are the days of the week, Monday through Friday, which are the same in singular and plural–*los lunes (Mondays), los martes (Tuesdays)* and so on.

Noun–Adjective Agreement

As in English, nouns in Spanish can be either singular or plural. But, unlike in English, adjectives in Spanish can also be singular or plural. Also, nouns in Spanish can be either masculine or feminine and so can adjectives.

The general rule of noun-adjective agreement in Spanish is simple: Singular nouns are accompanied by singular adjectives and plural nouns are accompanied by plural adjectives. Masculine nouns are described by masculine adjectives and feminine nouns are described by feminine adjectives. In other words, the adjectives chosen to describe nouns must match in both number and gender.

Generally, the 'normal' form of adjectives, the form you will find listed in dictionaries, is singular and masculine. To make the adjective plural, follow one of these steps:

- If it ends in an unstressed vowel, add -*s*. Examples: *verde* ('*green*', *singular*), *verdes* ('*green*', *plural*). *El árbol es verde*, the tree is green. *Los árboles son verdes*, the trees are green.

- If it ends in a *z*, change the *z* to a *c* and add *-es*. Example: *feliz* ('happy', *singular*), *felices* ('*happy*', *plural*).

Soy feliz, I'm a happy person; *somos felices*, we are happy people.

- If it ends in another consonant or a stressed vowel, add *-es*. Example: *difícil* (*'difficult'*, *singular*), *difíciles* (*'difficult'*, *plural*). *La tarea es difícil*, the task is difficult; *las tareas son difíciles*, the tasks are difficult.

- Note that in some cases it is necessary to add or remove an accent mark to maintain the stress on the correct syllable.

Making a masculine adjective feminine is even easier. Just follow these steps:

- If the singular masculine adjective ends in an *-o*, change it to an *-a*. Example: *pequeño* (*'small'*, *masculine singular*), *pequeña* (*'small'*, *feminine singular*). *El gato es pequeño*, the cat is small; *los gatos son pequeños*, the cats are small; *la chica es pequeña*, the girl is small; *las chicas son pequeñas*, the girls are small.

- If the singular masculine adjective ends in any other letter, the feminine form is the same. *El autobús es grande*, the bus is big; *la casa es grande*, the house is big.

As you will learn elsewhere, adjectives can come before or after nouns or they can be used with verbs such as *ser* ('to be') to describe nouns. But (*except for invariable adjectives*) they will always match the nouns they describe in both number and gender.

Important note: Invariable adjectives don't change in form and are very rare. Most of them are either uncommon colours or words of foreign origin. An example is *web* as in *la página web* (*the web page*) and *las páginas web* (*the web pages*). As a beginner you will seldom have the need to use invariable adjectives, but you should be aware that they exist so that they don't confuse you when you see them.

Lesson 5

Pronouns

Almost all of us like to take shortcuts and that's one way to think about what pronouns are: they're usually a shorter and quicker way of referring to a noun. Common pronouns in English include 'he', 'she', 'what', 'that' and 'yours', all of which often would be replaced by longer words or more words if we didn't have the pronouns at our disposal.

In general, pronouns in Spanish function much as they do in English. They can fulfil any role in a sentence that a noun can and some of them vary in form depending on whether they're used as a subject or an object. Probably the biggest difference is that in Spanish most pronouns have gender, whereas in English the only ones that do are those that refer specifically to males or females.

If a pronoun has gender, it is the same as the noun to which it refers and they are nearly always masculine or feminine. There are also a few neuter pronouns that can be used to refer to an unknown object or to ideas or concepts.

The chart below shows the different types of pronouns.

Type of pronoun	**Purpose**	**Examples in *Spanish* (English)**
Subject	Simply replaces the subject of a sentence	***Yo*** (*I*), ***tú*** (*you*), ***él*** (*he*), ***ella*** (*she*), ***ellos*** (*they*), ***ellas*** (*they*)
Demonstrative	Replaces a noun while also pointing to it	***Éste*** (*this one*), ***ésta*** (*this one*), ***ésa*** (*that one*), ***aquéllos*** (*those ones*)
Object	Functions as the object of a verb or preposition	***El*** (*him*), ***ella*** (*her*), ***mí*** (*me*), ***me*** (*me*), ***ellos*** (*them*)
Reflexive	Used when the direct object and indirect object of a verb refer to the same person. These are used much more in Spanish than in English.	***Me*** (*myself*), ***te*** (*yourself*), ***se*** (*himself, herself, themselves*)
Possessive	Refers to something owned or possessed by someone	***Mío*** (*mine*), ***mía*** (*mine*), ***míos*** (*mine*), ***mías*** (*mine*), ***suyo*** (*his, hers, theirs*)
Indefinite	Refers to nonspecific people or things	***Algo*** (*something*), ***nadie*** (*nobody*), ***alguien*** (*anybody*), ***todo*** (*all*), ***todas*** (*all*),

		uno (*one*), ***unos*** (*some*), ***ninguno*** (*none*)
Relative	Introduces a clause that gives more information about a noun or pronoun	***Que*** (*that, which, who, whom*), ***quien*** (*who, whom*), ***cuyo*** (whose), ***cuyas*** (*whose*), ***donde*** (*where*), ***lo cual*** (*which*)
Interrogative	Used in questions	***Qué*** (*what*), ***quién*** (*who*), ***cuándo*** (*when*)

Formal and Informal You

How do you say 'you' in Spanish? If you're new to learning Spanish, the answer isn't as simple as it may appear.

That's because Spanish, like many other languages, has several different ways that you can address other people, all of which can be translated by the English word 'you'.

First and most obvious, there are singular and plural forms, which aren't distinguished in the English word, although we can usually tell which is meant. But more important to learning how the Spanish language is used, Spanish also has formal and informal (also called 'familiar') ways of saying 'you', the usage depending on the person you're talking to and/or the circumstances. The difference doesn't come across in translating to English, but if you use the informal 'you' where the formal is required, you run the risk of sounding presumptuous or even arrogant.

First, here is a chart showing the various ways of saying 'you' as the subject of a sentence:

tú (singular informal) ***usted*** (singular formal)

vosotros (plural informal) ***ustedes*** (plural formal)

One reason for knowing which form to use is that there are corresponding words for 'your' and 'yours' as well as for 'you' when it isn't the subject of a sentence. Also, Spanish uses different verb forms for the informal and formal usages, with the informal forms taking a second-person conjugation while the formal forms take a third-person conjugation (the same used for the equivalents of 'he', 'she', and 'they').

The basic rule

As a general rule–although keep in mind that there are exceptions–when speaking with one person you can use the informal forms under roughly the same circumstances where you can use a person's first name in English.

More specifically, the singular informal *tú* is used when speaking with family members, children, pets, friends or close acquaintances, while *usted* is used when speaking with others. In most types of Christianity, at least, *tú* also is used when addressing God in prayer. *Tú* can also be used contemptuously when speaking to a stranger.

Obviously, the use of *tú* suggests a certain amount of intimacy. But the degree of intimacy varies with region. In some places, people of similar social status will start using *tú* upon meeting, while in other areas doing so might seem presumptuous. If you're uncertain which to use, it is usually better to use *usted* unless and until the person starts speaking to you using *tú*, in which case it is usually OK to reciprocate (unless you're a child or the person speaking to you is a police officer or other authority figure).

Lesson 6

Adjective

Demonstrative Adjectives

Demonstrative adjectives are those adjectives whose function is to point at something. In English, the singular demonstrative adjectives are 'this' and 'that', while the plural ones are 'these' and 'those'. *(Some grammarians refer to them as demonstrative determiners.)*

Unlike English, Spanish has three sets of demonstrative adjectives, which vary by number and gender, so there are 12 in all, as shown in the chart below. Translations are included in parentheses.

root word	singular masculine	plural masculine	singular feminine	plural feminine
este	***este*** *(this)*	***estos*** *(these)*	***esta*** *(this)*	***estas*** *(these)*
ese	***ese*** *(that)*	***esos*** *(those)*	***esa*** *(that)*	***esas*** *(those)*
aquel	***aquel*** *(that)*	***aquellos*** (those)	***aquella*** (that)	***aquellas*** (those)

Note that the masculine singular forms end in *-e*, not *-o*.

The demonstrative adjectives typically are placed before the nouns they modify. They must match the noun in both number and gender.

Examples

Me gusta este perro. (I like this dog.) Prefiero estas computadoras. (I prefer these computers.) Voy a comprar ese coche. (I'm going to buy that car.) Me gustan aquellas casas. (I like those houses.)

Although both *ese* and *aquel* and their related forms can be translated as 'that' or 'those', there are some distinctions in meaning. *Ese* and its related forms are more common and you're generally safe to use them when in English you'd use 'that' or 'those'. However, *aquel* and its related forms refer to something that's farther away in terms of distance or time. Although *ese* and its forms can be used for an object near the speaker or listener, *aquel* cannot. The distinction can be translated in a number of different ways, as the examples indicate.

Examples

Me gustan esos perros. (I like those dogs.) Me gustan aquellos perros. (I like those dogs over there.) No quiero esa casa. Quiero aquella casa. (I don't want that house. I want that house farther back.) ¿Recuerdas esos días? (Do you remember those days?) ¿Recuerdas aquellos días? (Do you remember those days long ago?)

When two or more items are in a series, the demonstrative adjective must be used with each item. While in English we would say 'those cats and dogs', in Spanish we would say *esos perros y esos gatos*.

Use of just one demonstrative adjective, as in *esos perros y gatos*, would imply that we're talking about animals that are a cross between a cat and a dog.

Possessive Adjectives (Short Form)

Possessive adjectives in Spanish, like those of English, are a way of indicating who owns or is in possession of something. Their use is straightforward, although they *(like other adjectives)* must match the nouns they modify in both number and gender.

Unlike English, Spanish has two forms of possessive adjectives, a short-form that is used before nouns and a long-form that is used after nouns. Long-form possessive adjectives will be explained later; here are the short-form possessive adjectives *(sometimes known as possessive determiners):*

mi, mis	my	*Compra **mis** libros. (He is buying **my** books.)*
tu, tus	your *(singular familiar)*	*Quiero comprar **tu** coche. (I want to buy **your** car.)*
su, sus	your *(singular or plural formal)*, its, his, her, their	*Voy a **su** oficina. (I am going to **his/her/your/ their** office.)*
nuestro, nuestra, nuestros, nuestras	our	*Es **nuestra** casa. (It is our house.)*
vuestro, vuestra, vuestros, vuestras	your *(plural familiar)*	*¿Dónde están **vuestros** hijos? (Where are **your** children?)*

Note that the possessive adjectives vary by number and gender. The change is with the nouns they modify, not with the person(s) who own or possess the object.

Examples

*Es **nuestro** coche. (It is **our** car.) Es **nuestra** casa. (It is **our** house.) Son **nuestros** coches. (They are **our** cars.) Son **nuestras** casas. (They are **our** houses.)*

As you might imagine, *su* and *sus* can be ambiguous, since they can mean 'his', 'her', 'its', 'your' or 'their'. If the use of *su* or *sus* doesn't make the sentence clear, you can use *de* followed by a prepositional pronoun.

Examples

*Quiero comprar **su** casa. (I want to buy **his/her/your/their** house.) Quiero comprar la casa **de él**. (I want to by **his** house.) Quiero comprar la casa **de ella**. (I want to by **her** house.) Quiero comprar la casa **de usted**. (I want to buy **your** house.) Quiero comprar la casa **de ellos.*** I want to buy **their** house.

In some areas, *de él*, *de ella* and *de ellos* are preferred over *su* and *sus* for saying 'his', 'her' and 'their', even where no ambiguity is present.

Overuse of the possessive adjectives

The possessive adjectives are used in most cases in the same way as they are used in English. However, you should be aware that in many instances–especially when speaking of body parts, clothing and items intimately associated with an individual–Spanish uses the definite article (*el*, *la*, *los* or *las*), the equivalent of 'the', instead of possessive adjectives.

Examples

Sam arregla el pelo. (Sam is combing his hair.) Ella juntó las manos para orar. (She joined her hands to pray.) Ricardo rompió los anteojos. (Ricardo broke his glasses.)

Repetition of possessive adjectives

In English, its common to use a single possessive adjective to refer to more than one noun. In Spanish, a single posessive adjective can refer to only one noun, unless the multiple nouns refer to the same persons or objects. For example, *son **mis** amigos y hermanos* would mean 'they are **my** friends and siblings (referring to the same people)', while *son **mis** amigos y **mis** hermanos* would mean 'they are **my** friends and siblings *(referring to different people)'*. Similarly, '**my** cats and dogs' would be translated as ***mis** gatos y **mis** perros.*

Possessive Adjectives (Long Form)

Unlike English, Spanish has two forms of possessive adjectives, a short-form that is used before nouns and a long-form that is used after nouns. Short-form possessive adjectives are explained before. Following are the long-form possessive adjectives with examples of usage:

mío, mía, míos, mías	my, of mine	*Son libros **míos**. (They are **my** books. They are books **of mine**.)*
tuyo, tuya, tuyos, tuyas	your *(singular familiar)*, of yours	*Prefiero la casa **tuya**. (I prefer **your** house. I prefer the house **of yours**.)*
suyo, suya, suyos, suyas	your *(singular or plural formal)*, its, his, her,	*Voy a la oficina **suya**. (I am going to **his/her/ your/their** office. I am*

	their, of yours, of his, of hers, of theirs	*going to the office* ***of his/hers/yours/ theirs****.)*
nuestro, nuestra, nuestros, nuestras	our, of ours	*Es un coche* ***nuestro****.* (It is **our** car. It is a car **of ours**.)
vuestro, vuestra, vuestros, vuestras	your (plural familiar), of yours	*¿Dónde están los hijos* ***vuestros****?* (Where are **your** children? Where are the children **of yours**?)

As you may have noticed, the short-form and long-forms of *nuestro* and *vuestro* and related pronouns are identical. They differ only as to whether they are used before or after the noun.

Note that the possessive adjectives vary by number and gender. The change is with the nouns they modify, not with the person(s) who own or possess the object.

Es un amigo ***tuyo****.* (He is a friend **of yours**.) *Es una amiga* ***tuya****.* (She is a friend **of yours**.) *Son unos amigos* ***tuyos****.* (They are some friends **of yours**.) *Son unas amigas* ***tuyas****.* (They are some friends **of yours**.)

If you've already studied possessive pronouns, you may have noticed that they are identical with the possessive adjectives listed above. In fact, some grammarians consider the possessive adjectives to actually be pronouns.

Choice of possessive form

Generally speaking, there is little or no difference in meaning between the long and short-forms of the possessive. Most often, you'd use the long-form as the equivalent of 'of mine', 'of yours', etc., in English, although (as in English) they are usually interchangeable in meaning. The short-form is more common and in some cases, the long-form can be somewhat awkward or have a slight 'literary' flavour, although it is used in informal speech as well.

Indefinite Adjectives

Indefinite adjectives are a loosely defined group of nondescriptive adjectives that are used to refer to noun whose specific identity isn't made. If that definition makes. little sense, see the list below for the English equivalents of these adjectives.

Like most other adjectives, indefinite adjectives match the nouns they refer to in both number and gender. They typically are placed before the noun they refer to. You should be aware that most of the indefinite adjectives can also be used as other parts of speech, most often pronouns and adverbs.

Here are the most common indefinite adjectives:

Adjective	**Meaning**	**Examples translations**	**Notes**
algún, alguna, algunos, algunas	some, a few, *any*	*Algún día voy a España. (Some day, I'm going to Spain.) Tiene algunos libros.* (He has some books.)	
cada	each, every	*Cada día voy a la oficina.* (I go to the office every day.)	*Cada* is invariable, making no changes with

		Tenemos un libro por cada tres estudiantes. (We have one book for every three students.)	number and gender.
cierto, cierta, ciertos, ciertas	a certain, specific	*Quiero comprar cierto libro. (I want to buy a certain book.) Ciertas estudiantes fueron a la biblioteca. (Certain students went to the library.)*	This adjective is not preceded by *un* or *una*. When used after a noun, the word means 'true' or 'right'.
cualquier, cualquiera	any, whatever, whichever, whoever,	*Cualquier estudiante puede aprobar el examen. (Any student can pass the test.) Estudia a cualquiera hora. (He studies at whatever*	A plural form, *cualesquiera (both masculine and feminine)* exists but is seldom used. When *cualquiera*

		time.) Podemos viajar a una ciudad cualquiera. (We can travel to any old city.)	(masculine or feminine) is used after the noun, it emphasises that the specific identity of the noun is unimportant, somewhat like 'any old' in English.
ningún, ninguna	no, not any	*No quiero ningún libro. (I don't want any books.) Ninguna mujer puede salir. (No woman can leave.)*	As in the first example, a 'double negative' can be required in Spanish when this adjective is used before the object of a verb. Plural forms (*ningunos*

			and *ningunas*) exist but are seldom used.
otro, otra, otros, otras	another, other	*Quiero otro lápiz. (I want another pencil.) Otra persona lo haría. (Another person would do it.) Quiero comprar los otros libros. (I want to buy the other books.)*	This adjective is not preceded by *un* or *una.*
todo, toda, todos, todas	each, every, all, all of	*Todo estudiante conoce a señor Smith. (Every student knows Mr. Smith.) Corrieron a toda velocidad. (They ran at full speed.) Todos los estudiantes conocen a señor Smith.*	When it means 'each' or 'every', *todo/toda* is used in singular form before the noun. When it means 'all of', the adjective precedes the entire noun

		(All of the students know Mr. Smith.) Durmió toda la noche. (She slept all night.)	phrase, as in the examples.
varios, varias	several	*Compró varios libros. (She bought several books.) Hay varias soluciones. (There are several solutions.)*	In singular form and sometimes in the plural form, the adjective also can mean 'varied', 'different' or 'various'.

Note that while some of these adjectives can be translated as 'any', the English word 'any' is often left untranslated into Spanish. *¿Tienen ustedes libros?* (Do you have any books?) *No tenemos libros. (We don't have any books.)*

Interrogative Adjectives

As their name suggests, interrogative adjectives are those adjectives that are used in questions. In Spanish, they take the same form as the interrogative pronouns, although only a few of the pronouns can be used as adjectives.

Qué

Qué is the most common interrogative pronoun and can be used to mean either 'what' or 'which' while referring to a noun. *Qué* does not change with number or gender.

Examples

*¿**Qué** zapato quisieras?* (**What** shoe would you like?) *¿**Qué** equipo ganó?* (**Which** team won?) *¿**Qué** personas van a salir?* (**What** people are going to leave?) *¿**Qué** coche prefieres?* (**Which** car do you prefer?)

Cuál

In parts of Latin America, but rarely in Spain and some other parts in Latin America, *cuál* can be used as an adjective to mean 'which' or 'what' and thus is interchangeable in some uses with *qué*. *Cuál* must match the noun it describes in number.

Examples

*¿**Cuáles** zapatos prefieres?* (**Which** shoes do you prefer?) *¿Mosquito? ¿**Cuál** mosquito?* (Mosquito? What mosquito?)

Cuánto

In singular form, *cuánto* or *cuánta* generally means 'how much' when referring to a singular noun; in plural form (*cuántos* or *cuántas*), it typically means 'how many'. It must match the noun it refers to in both number and gender.

Examples

*¿**Cuánto** dinero tienes?* (**How much** money do you have?) *¿**Cuánta** nata montada quisieras?* (**How much** whipped cream would you like?) *¿**Cuántos** años tiene él?* (How

old is he? *Literally*, **how many** years does he have?) *¿**Cuántas** jirafas hay?* (**How many** giraffes are there?)

Translating 'whose'

The English interrogative adjective 'whose' does not have an exact equivalent in Spanish. Although some thorough dictionaries list the word *cúyo (the interrogative form of cuyo)* that word is rarely used and is considered antiquated. The English 'whose' in questions is usually translated into Spanish using the phrase *de quién* or *de quiénes*, literally meaning 'of whom'.

Examples

¿De quién es este coche? (Whose car is this?) ¿De quiénes son esas casas? (Whose houses are those?)

Adjectives of Quantity

How many? How much? Unless you can answer with numbers, to respond to questions like that you'll probably need to use one of the adjectives of quantity.

Like most other nondescriptive adjectives, adjectives of quantity typically come before the noun they refer to *(just as in English)*. And like other adjectives, they must match the nouns they refer to in both number and gender.

Here are the most common adjectives of quantity with examples of how they are used:

Adjective	Translation	Examples	Notes
algún, alguna, algunos, algunas	some, any	*Alguna vez, voy al centro. (Some time, I will go downtown.) Pasaron*	Nearly all the time, the English 'any' in sentences such as the example is left

		algunos coches de policía. (Some police cars passed.) ¿Tienes algunos zapatos? (Do you have any shoes?)	untranslated into Spanish. For example, 'are there any watermelons?' becomes *¿hay sandías?*
ambos, ambas	both	*Ambas compañías crearán una empresa internacional. (Both companies will create an international enterprise.)*	
bastante, bastantes	enough, sufficient	*En mi ciudad hay bastantes iglesias. (In my city there are enough churches.)*	
mucho, mucha, muchos, muchas	much, many	*Los medios de comunicación tienen mucho poder.* (Communications media have	Typically, this word is translated as 'much' when singular and 'many' when plural.

		much power.) Ella tiene muchos gatos. *(She has many cats.)*	
ningún, ninguna	no	*Ninguna persona será atacada o ridiculizada. (No person will be attacked or ridiculed.)*	In Spanish, it is far less common to use *ninguno* or *ninguna* as an adjective than to use *no* as an adverb with the main verb, thus negating the entire sentence. Thus, 'I have no shoes' would typically be stated as *no tengo zapatos*.
poco, poca, pocos, pocas	small, little or slight; few	*Hay poco pan. (There is little bread.) Hay pocas uvas. (There are a few grapes.)*	As an adverb, *poco* can mean 'not'. For example, *es poco inteligente (he's unintelligent).*

suficiente	enough, sufficient	*Tenemos equipos suficientes para las inspecciones. (We have enough teams for the inspections.)*	*Bastante* is more commonly used than *suficiente.*
tanto, tanta, tantos, tantas	so much, so many	*Jamás había comido tanto queso. (He had never eaten so much cheese.) En América Latina nunca han existido tantos pobres como ahora.* (In Latin America there never have existed so many poor people as now.)	
todo, toda, todos, todas	each, every, all	*Todo americano lo sabe. (Every American knows it.) Todos los perros van al cielo. (All dogs go*	Use of *todo* or *toda* in singular form as an adjective isn't particularly common. *Todos* or *todas* is quite often used in

		to heaven.)	plural form before the definite article, as in the example.
unos, unas	some	*Unos gatos son mejores cazadores que otros. (Some cats are better hunters than others.)*	
varios, varias	several	*Javier tenían varios coches. (Javier had* Several cars.)	In some contexts, *varios* can mean 'various', and in that case is. sometimes placed after the noun.

Note that many of these adjectives are frequently used as other parts of speech, especially pronouns and adverbs.

Word Order of Adjectives

It is often said that adjectives come after nouns in Spanish. But this isn't entirely true–some types of adjectives frequently or always come before the nouns they modify and some can be placed either before or after nouns. Often, the determining factor in an adjective's placement is its purpose in the sentence.

Beginners usually don't have much difficulty with the placement of numbers, indefinite adjectives (words like *cada*/'each' and *algunos*/'some') and adjectives of quantity (such as *mucho*/'much' and *pocos*/'few'), which precede nouns in both languages. The main difficulty facing beginners is with descriptive adjectives. Students often learn that they are placed after the noun (which they usually are), but then they are surprised to find when they're reading 'real' Spanish outside their textbooks that adjectives are often used before the nouns they modify.

Tip for beginners

Most of the material in this Chapter is more appropriate for intermediate students than for beginners. If you're new to learning Spanish, it isn't important at this point to memorise the rules. What is important to remember is that while descriptive adjectives usually follow the nouns they modify, if one appears before the noun in something written or said by a native speaker it's probably not a mistake and there is probably a reason why the adjective is where it is.

Most of the words we think of as adjectives are descriptive adjectives, words that impart a quality of some sort to the noun. Most of them can appear either before or after a noun and here is the general rule for where:

After the noun

If an adjective **classifies** a noun that is, if it is used to distinguish that particular person or object from others that could be represented by the same noun, it is placed after the noun. Adjectives of color, nationality and affiliation (such as of religion or political party) usually fit in this category, as do many others. A grammarian might say in these cases that the adjective **restricts** the noun.

Before the noun

If the main purpose of the adjective is to **reinforce the meaning** of the noun, to **impart emotional effect** on the noun or to **convey appreciation** of some sort for the noun, then the adjective often is placed before the noun. A grammarian might say these are adjectives used **nonrestrictively**. Another way of looking at it is that placement before the noun often indicates a subjective quality (one dependent on the view of the person speaking) rather than an objective *(demonstrable)* one.

Keep in mind that this is a general rule only and sometimes there is no discernible reason for a speaker's choice of word order. But you can see some of the common differences in usage in the following examples:

la luz fluorescente *(the fluorescent light)*	*Fluorescente* is a category or classification of light, so it follows *luz*.
un hombre mexicano (a Mexican man)	*Mexicano* serves to classify *un hombre*.
La blanca nieve estaba por todas partes. (The white snow was everywhere.)	*Blanca (white)* reinforces the meaning of *nieve (snow)* and could also impart an emotional effect.
Es un ladrón condenado. (He is a convicted thief.)	*Condenado* (convicted) distinguishes the *ladrón* (thief) from others and is an objective quality.
¡Condenada computadora! Blasted computer!	*Condenada* is used for emotional effect, making it emphatically subjective. For this

reason, most vulgar adjectives of disparagement precede the nouns they describe.

To see how word order could make a difference, examine the following two sentences:

- *Me gusta tener un césped verde. (I like having a green lawn.)*
- *Me gusta tener un verde césped. (I like having a green lawn.)*

The difference between these two sentences is subtle and not readily translated. Depending on the context, the first might be translated as 'I like having a green lawn (*as opposed to a brown one*)', while the second might be translated as 'I like having a green lawn (as opposed to not having a lawn)'. In the first sentence, the placement of *verde* (green) after *césped* (lawn) indicates a classification. In the second sentence *verde*, by being placed first, reinforces the meaning of *césped* and indicates some aesthetic appreciation.

The effects of word order indicate why some adjectives are translated into English differently depending on their location. For example, *un amigo viejo* usually is translated as 'a friend who is old', while *un viejo amigo* is usually translated as 'a longtime friend', indicating some emotional appreciation. Similarly, *un hombre grande* is usually translated as 'a big man', while *un gran hombre* is 'a great man', indicating a subjective quality rather than an objective one. (*Grande*, when it precedes a masculine singular noun, is shorted to *gran*.) As you continue your studies, you will come across about another dozen adjectives that are similar.

Lesson 7

Adverbs

Like adjectives, adverbs are words that often are used to provide needed details in speech and writing. Although we could make grammatically complete sentences without them, we would be severely limited in what we could convey.

Spanish adverbs are much like their English counterparts. There are at least two ways in which you can define what adverbs are:

Words that tell us **when**, **how** or **where** the action or process in a sentence takes place.

Words that **modify** or **limit** the meaning of a **verb**, **adjective**, **adverb** or entire **sentence**.

A look at the examples below should make clear what types of words we're talking about.

As is the case in English, most adverbs are derived from adjectives, although there are some that are not. Separate Chapters here discuss each of those types in more detail.

Another way of classifying adverbs is by their function. Following are the most common types:

Adverbs of manner

Adverbs of manner are the most common and are used in a wide variety of situations, as they tell how something is done. In Spanish, they typically come after the verbs they modify.

Examples

Estudia **bien**. (She studies **well**.) *Canta* ***mal***. (*He sings* ***poorly***.) *Conduce* ***lentamente***. (*He drives* ***slowly***.) *Me abrazó* ***cariñosamente***. (She **affectionately** hugged me.) *Leo* ***mucho***. (I read **a lot**.)

Intensifiers and modifiers

These serve to make the adverb or adjective they modify either more or less intense. They come before the words they modify.

Examples

Estoy ***muy*** *cansada.* (*I am* ***very*** *tired.*) *Es* ***poco*** *inteligente.* (*He is* ***not very*** *intelligent.*) *Está* ***más*** *borracho.* (*He is quite drunk.*)

'Point of view' adverbs

These adverbs modify an entire sentence and evaluate it. Although they usually come at the beginning of a sentence, they don't have to.

Examples

Quizás él tenga miedo. (*Perhaps he is afraid.*) *Personalmente, no lo creo.* (*Personally, I don't believe it.*) *Pablo evidentemente estudia mucho.* (*Pablo obviously studies a lot.*)

Adverbs of time

These adverbs tell when something occurs. They often, but not always, come after the verb.

Examples

Salimos ***mañana.*** (*We're leaving* ***tomorrow.****) Nunca estudia.* (He **never** studies.)

Adverbs of place

These adverbs tell where an action or process occurs. They can be confusing for beginning learners, since many of the adverbs that indicate place can also function as prepositions or even as pronouns. Adverbs of place appear either before or after the verb they modify. It is perhaps even more important than in Spanish to make certain that the adverb is placed close to the verb it modifies.

Examples

Está ***aquí.*** (*It is* ***here.***) ***Allí*** *comeremos.* (*We'll eat* ***there.***) *Te busca* ***arriba.*** (*He is looking for you* ***upstairs.***)

Making Adverb from Adjectives

As in English, Spanish adverbs are words that modify or describe a verb, an adjective or another adverb. And, as in English, there are countless adverbs that can be created from adjectives and there is a fairly small number of adverbs that don't follow that pattern.

In English, adverbs can be created from many adjectives simply by adding '-ly' at the end. In Spanish, it's almost as easy.

The basic rule is that the suffix *-mente* is added to the end of the feminine, singular form of the adjective.

Generally, the feminine, singular form of the adjective is the same as the 'regular' or masculine, singular form unless the adjective ends in an *o*, in which case the *-o* is changed to an *-a*.

See the following examples:

Basic adjective	Singular, (feminine form)	Adverb
feliz (*happy*)	*feliz*	*felizmente* (*happily*)
fácil (*easy*)	*fácil*	*fácilmente* (*easily*)
alegre (*joyful*)	*alegre*	*alegremente* (*joyfully*)
nuevo (*new*)	*nueva*	*nuevamente* (*newly*)
rápido (*rapid*)	*rápida*	*rápidamente* (*rapidly*)

Note, as in two of the examples above that if an adjective has an accent mark, the corresponding adverb retains the accent mark, even though the spoken emphasis likely will be on the next-to-last syllable.

When two adverbs are used in a series, the *-mente* suffixed is dropped from all but the last adverb.

Habla lenta y claramente. She speaks slowly and clearly.

Anda cuidadosa, dificultosa y pacientemente. He walks carefully, with difficulty and patiently.

Adverbs not ending in –mente

Although many Spanish adverbs are derived from adjectives, just as they are in English, many are not. So, although you can recognise many Spanish adverbs by their *-mente* ending, many others, including some of the most common ones, need to be learned separately.

Such adverbs include certain adverbs of place (ones that tell where the verb's action takes place), intensifiers and moderators (ones that tell how much, *such as 'very'*), adverbs of time (ones that tell when) and adverbs of manner (ones that describe how).

Following are some of the most common adverbs that don't end in *-mente*, along with their approximate meanings and sample sentences. Note that many of the words on this list are frequently used as other parts of speech, especially adjectives, so you need to rely on the context to tell you if indeed the word is being used as an adverb.

ahí	there	*Duerme ahí.* He is sleeping there.
ahora	now	*Come ahora.* He's eating now.
algo	somewhat	*Está algo cansada.* She is somewhat tired.
allí	over there	*Duerme allí.* He is sleeping over there.
aquí	here	*Edison durmió aquí.* Edison slept here.
ayer	yesterday	*Trabajaba ayer.* He was working yesterday.
bastante	rather, sufficiently	*Corre bastante mal.* He runs rather badly.
bien	well	*Corres bien.* You run well.
demasiado	too	*Come demasiado rápido.* He eats too fast.
despacio	slowly	*Anda despacio.* He walks slowly.
mal	badly, poorly	*Corres mal.* You run poorly.
mañana	tomorrow	*Trabajaré mañana.* I will work tomorrow.

no	not	*No come.* He isn't eating.
nunca	never	*Nunca trabaja.* She never works.
mucho	a lot	*Habla mucho.* He talks a lot.
muy	very	*Estaba muy cansada.* She was very tired.
poco	a little, 'un-' or 'in-'	*Estudia poco.* He studies a little. *Este coche es poco económico.* This car is uneconomical.
nada	not at all	*Estudia nada.* He doesn't study at all.
siempre	always	*Siempre estudia.* She is always studying.
tan	so	*La vida es tan buena.* Life is so good.
ya	already, now	*Ya viene.* He's coming now.

Lesson 8

Prepositions

On the one hand, prepositions in Spanish are easy to understand, because they usually function in almost the same way as they do in English. On the other hand, prepositions can be one of the most challenging aspects of using Spanish, because it is not always easy to remember which preposition to use. A simple and very common preposition such as the Spanish *en* can be translated not only as 'in', the most common translation, but also as 'to', 'by' and 'about'.

A preposition is a type of word that is used to form a clause; the clause in turn functions as an adjective or adverb. In both English and Spanish, a preposition is followed by an object, which is usually a noun. The object also can be a pronoun or verb that functions as a noun. (Sometimes in English a preposition can appear at the end of a sentence, but that isn't done in Spanish.) If all this doesn't make clear to you what a preposition is, a look at the list below should make it clear what types of words we're talking about.

Let's look at a couple of sample sentences to see how the

preposition relates its object to other parts of a sentence.

I	am going	to	the store.
Yo	*voy*	*a*	*la tienda.*
Subject	verb	preposition	prepositional object

In the above sentence the phrase 'to the store' or *a la tienda* form a clause that functions as an adverb that complements the verb.

Here is an example of a prepositional clause that functions as an adjective:

I	see	the shoe	under	the table.
Yo	*veo*	*el zapato*	*bajo*	*la mesa.*
Subject	verb	direct object	preposition	prepositional object

In this case, 'under the table' is a clause which works as an adjective that describes the shoe.

Like English, Spanish has perhaps a few dozen prepositions. The following list shows the most common ones along with some of the most common meanings. Keep in mind that the translations below aren't exhaustive.

Common Spanish Prepositions

a	to, at, by means of	*Vamos a la ciudad.* We are going to the city. *Vengo a las tres.* I am coming at 3. *Viajamos a pie.* We are travelling by foot.

antes de	before	*Leo antes de dormirme.* I read before going to sleep.
bajo	under	*El perro está bajo la mesa.* The dog is under the table.
cerca de	near	*El perro está cerca de la mesa.* The dog is near the table.
con	with	*Voy con él.* I am going with him.
contra	against	*Estoy contra la huelga.* I am against the strike.
de	of, from, indicating possession	*El sombrero es hecho de papel.* The hat is made of paper. *Soy de Nueva York.* I'm from New York. *Prefiero el carro de Juan.* I prefer John's car (*I prefer the car of John*).
delante de	in front of	*Mi carro está delante de la casa.* My car is in front of the house.
dentro de	inside	*El perro está dentro de la jaula.* The dog is inside the cage.
desde	since, from	*No comí desde ayer.* I haven't eaten since yesterday. *Tiró el béisbol desde el carro.* He threw the baseball from the car.

después de	after	*Comemos después de la clase.* We are eating after class.
detrás de	behind	*El perro está detrás de la mesa.* The dog is behind the table.
durante	during	*Dormimos durante la clase.* We slept during the class.
en	in, on	*Ella está en Nueva York.* She is in New York. *El perro está en la mesa.* The dog is on the table.
encima de	on top of	*El gato está encima de la casa.* The cat is on top of the house.
enfrente de	in front of	*El perro está enfrente de la mesa.* The dog is in front of the table.
entre	beween	*El perro está entre le mesa y el sofá.* The dog is between the table and the sofa.
fuera de	outside of	*El perro está fuera de la casa.* The dog is outside of the house.
hacia	toward	*Caminamos hacia la escuela.* We are walking toward the school.
hasta	until	*Duermo hasta las seis.* I'm sleeping until 6.
para	for, in order to	*El regalo es para usted.*

		The gift is for you. *Trabajo para ser rico.* I work in order to be rich.
por	for, by	*Damos gracias por la comida.* We give thanks for the meal. *Fue escrito por Juan.* It was written by Juan.
según	according to	*Según el periódico, va a nevar.* According to the newspaper, it is going to snow.
sin	without	*Voy sin él.* I am going without him.
sobre	over, about	*Se cayó sobre la silla.* He fell over the chair. *Es un programa sobre el presidente.* It's a programme about the president.
tras	after, behind	*Caminaban uno tras otro.* The walked one after (*behind*) the other.

The Preposition A

As a beginner at learning Spanish, you may be told that the Spanish preposition *a* is the way of expressing the English preposition 'to'. Indeed, this is often the case. But it won't take you long to find out that *a* also has a wide variety of other uses. In fact, it can be translated not only as 'to', but also as 'on', 'at', 'from', 'by' or 'in' — or various other prepositions. And in many cases it is not translated at all.

Rather than learning how to use *a* by its translation, it is probably best to learn the **purposes** for which *a* is used. Look over the chart below for some examples of how *a* is commonly used. This chart doesn't cover all its uses, but it does show the uses you are most likely to come across at the beginning stages of learning Spanish. Where *a* is translated, the translation is indicated in boldface.

(**Note**: In a few places below you'll see the contraction *al*, which is short for *a + el*.)

Purpose	Comment	Examples	Translation
to indicate motion	Almost any verb indicating motion and even nouns, can be followed by *a* before the destination.	*Llegamos* ***a*** *St. Louis. Se acercó* ***a*** *la casa. Cayó* ***al*** *piso. Esa es la puerta* ***al*** *baño. Me siento* ***a*** *la mesa.*	We arrived **at** St. Louis. He got near the house. It fell **to** the floor. That is the door **to** the bathroom. I am sitting **at** the table.
to connect a verb with a following infinitive	This use of *a* is especially common following verbs indicating the start of an action.	*Empezó* ***a*** *salir. Entró a hablar contigo. Él se negó* ***a*** *nadar. He venido* ***a*** *estudiar. Comenzó* ***a*** *bailar. Voy* ***a*** *cantar.*	She began to leave. He came in to talk to you. He refused to swim. I have come to study. She began to dance. I am going to sing.
to indicate manner or method	Numerous expressions begin with *a* followed by a noun to	*Vamos* ***a*** *pie. Hay que fijarlo* ***a*** *mano. Estoy* ***a***	We are going **on** foot. It is necessary to fix it **by** hand. I am **on** a diet. I am

	indicate how something is done. The phrase starting with *a* functions as an adverb and is sometimes translated as on.	*dieta. Escribo* ***a*** *lápiz. Andan* ***a*** *ciegas. Llegamos* ***a*** *tiempo. Lee el libro* ***a*** *escondidas.*	writing with a pencil. They are walking blindly. We are arriving **on** time. He is studying the book covertly.
to introduce a direct object that is a person or treated like a person	This usage is known as the 'personal *a*'. The preposition in these cases usually is not translated.	*Conozco* ***a*** *Pedro. Encontré* ***a*** *Fido. Veré* ***a*** *María.*	I know Peter. I found Fido. I will see Mary.
to introduce an indirect object		*Le doy una camisa* ***a*** *Jorge. Compro una camisa* ***a*** *Jorge. Le robo una camisa* ***a*** *Jorge. Le pongo la camisa* ***a*** *Jorge.*	I am giving a shirt **to** George. I am buying a shirt **for** George. I am taking a shirt **from** George. I am putting the shirt **on** George.
in various expressions		*Salimos* ***a*** *las cuatro.*	We are leaving **at** four. Today is

of time	*Estamos **a** lunes.*	Monday.

Keep in mind that not all uses of *a* are listed here and that in some cases other prepositions can be used for the same purpose. As you become more familiar with Spanish, you will come to know instinctively which preposition to use in various circumstances.

The Preposition Con

Con (pronounced basically like the English 'cone', not like 'con') is one of the most common Spanish prepositions. The vast majority of the time, it is the equivalent of the English 'with', so it normally causes little confusion for the English speaker trying to learn Spanish.

The important thing to keep in mind about *con* is that it is somewhat more versatile than the English 'with', so you will run across many cases where *con* is used that you probably wouldn't use 'with' in English.

Here are some of the most common cases where *con* is used in a way that differs from the use of 'with' in English. Note that in many of the examples given, *con* could be understood to mean 'with', but it would be awkward to translate it that way.

With certain verbs, *con* is used where a different preposition (or none) is used in English. Such usages are unpredictable and need to be learned along with the verbs. *Es necesario **acabar con** el escándalo.* (It is necessary **to put an end to** the scandal.) *Para comer, **basta con** cinco dólares.* (*In order to eat, five dollars **is enough**.*) *El coche **chocó con** el tren.* (*The car **crashed into** the train.*) *Puedo **contar con** mis amigos.* (*I can **count on** my friends.*) *Tengo que **enfrentarme** el problema.* (*I have **to face up to** the problem.*) ***Me espanto con** las hormigas.*

(*I* ***am frightened of*** *ants.*) *Muchas veces* ***sueño con*** *la guerra.* (*I often* ***dream about*** *the war.*) *Quiero* ***tropezar con*** *mi madre* or *Quiero* ***encontrarme con*** *mi madre.* (*I want* ***to run into*** *my mother.*)

To form phrases that function like adverbs. The same can be done in English with 'with' and other prepositions, but it is much more common in Spanish; in some cases, such prepositional phrases are used in preference to or instead of synonymous adverbs.

Habla ***con intensidad***. (*He speaks* ***intensely***.) *Me preguntó* ***con cortesía***. (*He asked me* ***courteously***.) *Vive* ***con felicidad***. (*She lives* ***happily***.) *Anda* ***con prisa***. (*She walks* ***fast***.)

Sometimes when followed by an infinitive or a noun, *con* can have a variety of translations to indicate some sort of condition being met or not met. Such translations include 'if', 'despite' and 'by'. ***Con decirle*** *que no tengo dinero, todo estará bien.* (***By telling him*** *that I don't have money, everything will be fine.*) ***Con todo***, *no está enferma.* (***Despite everything***, *she's not sick.*) ***Con correr*** *puedes verla.* (***If you run*** *you can see her*).

Contractions: When *con* is followed by the pronoun *mí* or *ti* to say 'with me' or 'with you', the phrase is shorted to *conmigo* or *contigo*, respectively. **Examples:** *Ven* ***conmigo***. (*Come* ***with me***.) *Vendré* ***contigo***. (*I will come* ***with you***.)

The Preposition De

De is one of the most common prepositions in Spanish. Although it usually is translated as 'of', and sometimes as 'from', its use is far more versatile than the translation might suggest. In fact, in certain contexts, *de* can be translated not only as 'of' or 'from', but as 'with', 'by', or 'in', among other words or not translated at all.

One reason *de* is used more often than its equivalents in English is because the rules of English grammar let us use all sorts of nouns and phrases as adjectives. But in that way, Spanish isn't quite so flexible. While in English we may say, 'a nine-year-old girl', in Spanish that becomes *una muchacha de nueve años* or, literally, 'a girl of nine years'. Similarly, in English, we may say something like 'a silver ring', using what is normally a noun, 'silver', as an adjective. But in Spanish we have to say *un anillo de plata* or 'a ring of silver'.

De also is used in Spanish to indicate possession. We may talk about 'John's shoe' in English, but in Spanish it's *el zapato de Juan* or 'the shoe of John'.

Following are some of the most common uses of *de*:

Cause

Following an adjective, *de* can be used to indicate a cause. *Estoy feliz de nuestra amistad*, I am happy with our friendship; *está cansada de jugar*, she is tired of playing.

Origin

Often translated as 'from', *de* can be used to indicate the origin of a person or thing. *Soy de Arkansas*, I'm from Arkansas; *mi madre es de la India*, my mother is from India; *la chica más inteligente de la clase*, the most intelligent girl in the class.

Characteristics

When an object or person has characteristics (including contents or what something is made of) that are stated as a noun or infinitive, *de* is often used to show the relationship. It generally is not possible in Spanish, as it is in English, to use nouns as adjectives. *Corazón de oro*, heart of gold; *el tranvía de Boston*, the Boston streetcar; *una casa de huéspedes*, a guesthouse; *una canción de tres minutos*, a three-minute song; *una casa de $100,000*, a $100,000 house; *una taza de leche*, a cup of milk; *la mesa de escribir*, the writing table; *una casa de ladrillo*, a brick house; *jugo de manzana*, apple juice; *una máquina de escribir*, typewriter.

Comparisons

In some comparisons, *de* is used where we would use 'than' in English. *Tengo menos de cien libros*, I have fewer than 100 books; *gasta más dinero de lo que gana*, he spends more money than he earns.

Idioms

De is used in a number of idiomatic phrases, many of which function as adverbs. *De antemano*, previously; *de cuando en cuando*, from time to time; *de memoria*, by memory; *de moda*, in style; *de nuevo*, again; *de pronto*, suddenly; *de prisa*, hurriedly; *de repente*, suddenly; *de todas formas*, in any case; *de veras*, truly; *de vez en cuando*, from time to time.

Possession

Possession or belonging, either physical or figurative, as indicated by ''s' in English is almost always translated using *de* followed by the possessor in Spanish: *el carro de Matilda*, Matilda's car; *la clase de Sr. Gómez*, Mr. Gomez's class; *las esperanzas del pueblo*, the people's hopes; *¿De quién es este lápiz?* Whose pencil is this?

Verb expressions

Many verbs are followed by *de* and often an infinitive to

form expressions. *Acabo de salir*, I have just left; *nunca cesa de comer*, he never stops eating; *trataré de estudiar*, I will try to study; *me alegro de ganar*, I am happy to win; *se olvidó de estudiar*, he forgot to study; *Romeo se enamoró de Julieta*, Romeo fell in love with Juliet.

You will also occasionally see other uses of *de*, although those above are the most common. There are also many expressions and verb combinations using *de* that were not listed above.

Keep in mind also that when *de* is followed by the article *el*, meaning 'the', they form the contraction *del*. Thus *los árboles del bosque* is the equivalent of saying *los árboles de el bosque* ('the trees of the forest'). But no contraction is used for *de él*, which means 'his'.

The Preposition En

If you were told that *en* is a Spanish preposition and were asked what it means, you most likely would guess 'in' or 'on'. And you'd be right — in both cases. But *en* can also be translated as 'at', 'about', 'by', 'on top of', 'upon', 'inside of' and other ways, so its use isn't as straightforward as it may appear.

Fortunately, when *en* doesn't mean 'on' or 'in', you can usually tell by the context what is meant. Like some of the other prepositions, *en* can seem quite versatile to the foreigner. Here are the most common uses of *en* you're likely to run across:

Meaning	**Examples**
Indicating location and meaning 'in'	*El dinero está en la caja.* The money is in the box. *Vivo en España.* I live in Spain. (**Note:** *'In' meaning 'inside of' also can be expressed by dentro de.*)

Indicating time and meaning 'in'	*Llegamos en una hora.* We arrive in one hour. *Trabajaré en el verano.* I will work in the summer. (**Note:** *En isn't used with days of the week. Llegamos ellunes. We arrive on Monday.*)
Indicating location and meaning 'on'	*El dinero está en la mesa.* The money is on the table. *Fijó los carteles en la pared.* He put up the posters on the wall. (**Note**: The preposition *a* alternatively could have been used in the second sentence. *Fijó los carteles a la pared.*)
To express a value	*Vendió el carro en $2.000.* He sold the car for $2,000. (**Note:** *The preposition por alternatively could have been used in the previous sentence. Vendió el carro por $2.000.)*
In numerous expressions, with various meanings	*En broma*, as a joke; *en busca de*, in search of; *en cambio*, on the other hand; *en casa*, at home; *en español*, in Spanish; *en honor de*, in honour of; *en la actualidad*, presently; *en la radio*, on radio; *en la televisión (TV)*, on television (TV); *en lugar de*, instead of; *en secreto*, in secret; *en*

	seguida, immediately; *en serio*, seriously; *en todas partes*, everywhere; *en vez de*, instead of; *en vista de*, in view of; *en vivo*, live (as in live TV); *en voz alta*, in a loud voice; *en voz baja*, in a soft voice
With certain verbs to mean 'in' or 'on'	*Competir en*, to compete in; *concentrarse en*, to concentrate on; *concurrir en*, to concur in; *confiar en*, to trust in; *creer en*, to believe in; *empeñarse en*, to persist in; *esperar en*, to trust in; *insistir en*, to insist on; *intervenir en*, to participate in; *persistir en*, to persist in; *reflejar en*, to reflect on; *resultar en*, to result in
With certain verbs to have other meanings	*Adentrarse en*, to get into; *aplicarse en*, to work hard at *coincidir en que*, to agree that; *comprometerse en*, to get involved in; *concurrir en*, to meet in; *consentir en*, to agree to; *consistir en*, to be composed of; *convenir en*, to agree to; *convertir(se) en*, to be changed into; *equivocarse en*, to be mistaken about; *fijarse en*, to notice; *ingresar en*, to be admitted to; *molestarse en*, to bother to; *pensar en*, to think

about; *quedar en que*, to agree that; *reparar en*, to notice; *vacilar en*, to hesitate to

As a beginner, you don't need to memorise all the phrases and verbs that use *en*; of the verb phrases, *pensar en* (*to think about*) is the most common one that causes beginners difficulty. But you should be aware of those uses, so you know that *en* might not mean 'in' or 'on'.

The Preposition Para

Para is one of the most useful and common prepositions in Spanish, but it can also be one of the most confusing to English speakers. That is because it is usually translated as 'for', and so is the preposition *por* and they are very seldom interchangeable.

As a beginner, it is probably best to learn the two prepositions separately and to think of *para* as a preposition that usually indicates purpose or destination, rather than simply as a translation for 'for'. So in the examples of *para* usage that are given below, a translation (*sometimes awkward*) using a word or phrase other than 'for' is given, in addition to a translation using 'for'. By learning how *para* is used rather than how it is usually translated, you will find it easier to learn in the long run.

Here, then, are the most common uses of *para*:

To mean 'in order to'

When used in this way, it is followed by an infinitive.

Examples

Viajamos para aprender español. (*We travel in order to learn Spanish. We travel for learning Spanish.*) *Vive para comer.* (*He lives in order to eat. He lives for eating.*)

To indicate purpose, intent, usefulness or need

The preposition can be used quite flexibly in this regard, in many cases being used in such a a way that there is no simple one-word English equivalent.

Examples

Estudia para dentista. *(She is studying to become a dentist. She is studying for the dental profession.)* Quisiera una bicicleta para dos. *(I'd like a bicycle for two. I'd like a bicycle made with the intent that two people use it.)* Es hecho para niños. *(It is made for children. It is made to be used by children.)* El poema fue escrito para su esposa. *(The poem was written for his wife. The poem was written with his wife as the intended recipient.)* Feliz cumpleaños para ti. *(Happy birthday to you. Happy birthday for you.)* Tenemos agua para una semana. *(We have water for a week. We have water enough to last a week.)* ¿Para qué estudias? *(Why do you study? For what purpose do you study?)*

To indicate a destination

This is a specific way of indicating intention. In some of these cases, *para* can be used interchangeably with *a*, meaning 'to'.

Examples

Salimos para Londres. (We are leaving to go to London. We are leaving for London.) *No voy para casa.* (I am not going home. I am not headed for home.) *¿Para dónde va el taxi?* (*Where does the taxi go to*?)

To mean 'no later than' or 'by'

As can be seen by the examples, this is another way of indicating intent. In some contexts, *para* can mean '**around**' or 'about' a certain time.

Examples

La casa estará lista para el sábado. (The house will be ready no later than Saturday. The house will be ready by Saturday. The house will be ready for Saturday.) *La casa estará lista para la boda.* (The house will be ready by the wedding. The house will be ready before the wedding. The house will be ready for the wedding.) *Llegamos para las cinco.* (*We're arriving around 5. We're arriving about 5.*)

To mean 'considering' or 'in view of':

Examples

Para niño, es inteligente. (*Considering that he's a child, he's intelligent. For a child, he's intelligent.) Es caro para un papel.* (It's expensive in view of the fact it's a sheet of paper. It's expensive for a sheet of paper.)

To indicate a personal reaction

Examples

Para ella, es difícil. (*To her, it's difficult. For her, it's difficult.*) *No es justo para mí.* (*It isn't right to me. It doesn't seem right to me. It isn't right for me.*)

With* estar *to mean 'to be about to' or 'to be ready to'

This phrase is followed by the infinitive.

Examples

Estoy para salir. (I'm ready to leave. I am about to leave.) *Estamos para hacer negocios.* (*We're ready to do business. We're ready for doing business.*)

The Preposition Por

Por is one of the most useful and common prepositions in Spanish, but it can also be one of the most confusing to English speakers. That is because it is sometimes translated as 'for', as is the preposition *para* and they are very seldom interchangeable.

As a beginner, it is probably best to learn the two prepositions separately and to think of *por* as a preposition that usually indicates cause or motive, rather than simply as a translation for 'for'. (*It also often means 'by', but it isn't the only Spanish preposition translated that way.*) So in the examples of *por* usage that are given below, a translation (sometimes awkward) using a word or phrase other than 'for' is given, in addition to a translation using 'for' (*where appropriate*). By learning how *por* is used rather than how it is usually translated, you will find it easier to learn in the long-run.

Here, then, are the most common uses of *por*:

To indicate the cause of or reason for something

In such usages, *por* can often be translated as 'because of'.

Examples

¿Por qué? (Why? Because of what? For what?) *Trabajo aquí por el dinero.* (*I work here because of the money. I work here for the money.*) *No podemos salir por la lluvia.* (*We cannot leave because of the rain. We cannot leave due to the rain.*) *Conseguí el empleo por mi padre.* (*I got the job because of my father. I got the job through my father.*)

To indicate support of or action on behalf of some person or cause:

Examples

Voto por Julia González. (I am voting for Julia Gonzales. I am voting in support of Julia Gonzalez.) Es socio de Médicos Por Justicia. (He is a member of Doctors for Justice. He is a member of Doctors Supporting Justice.) Mi padre está por no violencia. (*My father is for nonviolence. My father is a supporter of nonviolence.*) Es el representante por el estado de Nueva York. (He's the representative for the state of New York. He's the representative on behalf of the state of New York.)

To indicate an exchange of some sort

One common use of this type is indicating how much something cost.

Examples

Compré el coche por 10.000 dólares.(I bought the car for $10,000. I bought the car in exchange for $10,000.) *Gracias por la comida.* (Thanks for the meal.) *Quisiera cambiar la camisa por una nueva.* (I'd like to exchange the shirt for a new one.)

To indicate being in a place

In such uses, *por* doesn't indicate a destination, but rather proximity or placement. It is often translated as 'by' or 'through'.

Examples

Pasaremos por San Francisco. (We will pass through San Francisco.) La escuela no está por aquí. (The school isn't near here.)

As a translation for 'per'

In informal contexts, a translation of 'for' rather than

'per' is common in English.

Examples

El tres por ciento tiene dos coches. (*Three per cent have two cars.*) *Compré dos regalos por persona.* (*I bought two gifts per person. I bought two gifts for each person.*) *Trabajo 40 horas por semana.* (*I work 40 hours per week. I work 40 hours a week.*)

To mean 'by' when it points to someone performing an action

Common uses are indicating the author of a book or other work or indicating the performer of a passive verb.

Examples

Fue escrito por William Shakespeare. (*It was written by William Shakespeare.*) *Los tacos fueron comidos por los estudiantes.* (The snacks were eaten by the students.) *Prefiero el libro por Isaac Asimov.* (I prefer the book by Isaac Asimov.) *Puedo estudiar por sí mismo.* (I can read all by myself.)

In certain set phrases

Such phrases are commonly used as adverbs. The meaning of such phrases isn't always obvious by translating the words individually.

Examples

por cierto (certainly), *por lo general* (generally), *por supuesto* (of course), *por otra parte* (on the other hand), *por fin* (finally), *por lo menos* (at least).

Lesson 9

Comparison of Inequalities

Not only is it possible to describe someone as happy, it is also possible to describe that happiness is various degrees–happier, happier than someone, happiest, as happy as someone. In this Chapter, we learn how to express the first two of those alternatives.

In English, we usually can make an adjective stronger by adding '-er' to the end (such as in 'happier', 'stronger' and '*faster*') or by using it with the word 'more' (*as in 'more considerate' and 'more intense'*). In Spanish, there is no direct equivalent of '-er'; adjectives are made more intense by preceding them with *más*.

Examples

María está más feliz. María is happier. *El cielo de Chile es más azul.* Chile's sky is bluer. *Mis padres son más ricos.* My parents are richer. *Compro unos libros más caros.* I am buying some more expensive books.

Usually, the word *que* is used when making a comparison.

Examples

Mi coche es más grande que tu coche. My car is bigger than your car. *Soy más alto que tú.* I'm taller than you. *La casa es más blanca que la nieve.* The house is whiter than the snow.

To indicate 'less' rather than 'more', use *menos.*

Examples

María está menos feliz. María is less happy. *El cielo de Chile es menos azul.* Chile's sky is less blue. *La casa es menos blanca que la nieve.* The house is less white than the snow.

Más and *menos* can be used with adverbs in the same way.

Examples

Corres más rápido que yo. You run faster than I. *Silvia habla menos claramente que Ana.* Silvia speaks less clearly than Ana.

Exceptions

There are a few exceptions to the above rules.

Adjective/adverb	**Comparative**	**Example**
bueno, buena (good)	*mejor* (better)	*Eres mejor hombre que yo.* You are a better man than I.
bien (*well*)	*mejor* (*better*)	*Ella estudia mejor que tú.* She studies better than you.
malo, mala (bad)	*peor* (*worse*)	*Mi bicicleta es*

		peor. My bicycle is worse.
mal (badly)	*peor (worse)*	*Se siente peor que yo.* He feels worse than I.

Additionally, although *más pequeño* and *más grande* are often used for 'smaller' and 'bigger', respectively, *menor* and *mayor* are sometimes used. *Mayor* also is used to mean 'older' when referring to people.

Do not confuse comparisons of adjectives or adverbs with 'more than' and 'less than' in the following examples. Note that *más de* and *menos de* are used when referring to numbers.

Examples

Tengo más de 30 pesos. I have more than 30 pesos. *Mi hijo tiene menos de 20 años.* My son is less than 20 years old.

Lesson 10

Plurals

In Latin America, the informal plural, *vosotros*, is seldom used, even when talking with family members, so *ustedes* is used in plural cases. In Spain, *vosotros* is generally used as the plural of *tú*.

The pronoun vos

In some parts of Latin America, the pronoun *vos* replaces or partly replaces *tú*, especially in spoken Spanish. In some areas, *vos* implies even greater intimacy than *tú* does and in some other areas it has its own verb forms. As a foreigner, however, you're perfectly safe using *tú* even where *vos* is common.

Subject Pronouns: Their usage and omissions

Subject pronouns in Spanish are a lot like medicine–they're often essential, but their use should be avoided when they're not necessary.

Overuse of subject pronouns–the equivalent of words such as 'he', 'she' and 'they'–is common among English speakers learning Spanish. It's important to remember that in Spanish the verb forms often make subject pronouns unnecessary and when that's the case the pronouns shouldn't be used unless there's a reason to.

Here is a sampling of sentences where pronouns are unnecessary:

Voy al supermercado. I am going to the supermarket. (The verb *voy* can refer only to the person speaking.)

¿Dónde vas? Where are you going? (The verb *vas* necessarily refers to the person being spoken to.)

Roberto no está en casa. ¿Fue al supermercado? Roberto isn't at home. Did he go to the supermarket? (Standing alone, the second sentence might be unclear about who the subject is. But in context, it is obvious that Roberto is being referred to.)

Nieva. *It is snowing.*

Of course, not all sentences will be as clear as those are without explicit reference to the subject. Here are the subject pronouns in Spanish with their English equivalents:

yo	I
tú	you (informal singular)
usted	you (formal singular)
él, ella	he, she
nosotros, nosotras	we (the first form refers to a group of males or males and females, while the second form refers to females only)

vosotros, vosotras	you (informal plural; the first form refers to a group of males or males and females, while the second form refers to females only)
ustedes	you (formal plural)
ellos, ellas	they (the first form refers to a group of males or males and females, while the second form refers to females only)

Note that there is no pronoun listed for 'it' as a subject; in sentences where we'd use the subject 'it' in English, the use of the third-person verb makes a pronoun unnecessary. Although Spanish does have a rarely heard pronoun meaning 'it', *ello*, its use is limited mainly to literature and it isn't used to refer to named objects.

Using subject pronouns

Subject pronouns are used in the following instances:

To avoid ambiguity

Context doesn't always make clear who the subject is and some verb forms are ambiguous. *Yo tenía un coche.* I had a car. (Out of context, *tenía* could mean 'I had', 'you had', 'he had' or 'she had'. If the context makes the subjects clear, the pronouns normally wouldn't be used.) *Juan y María son alumnos. Él estudia mucho.* John and Mary are students. He studies a lot. (Without the pronoun, it is impossible to tell whom the second sentence refers to.)

For emphasis

In English, unlike Spanish, we often use verbal stress to emphasise a pronoun. For example, if a strong emphasis is placed on the 'I' in '**I** am going to the supermarket', the understood meaning of the sentence might be 'I (and not somebody else) am going to the supermarket' or possibly 'I am going to the supermarket (and I'm proud of myself)'. In Spanish, one could similarly add an emphasis by using the grammatically unnecessary pronoun: *Yo voy al supermercado.* Similarly, *tú haz lo que tú quieres* could be understood as '**you** do what **you** want (and see if I care)'.

Change of subject

When contrasting two subjects, the pronouns are frequently used. *Yo estudio y él escucha el estéreo.* I'm studying and he's listening to the stereo. *Nosotros somos pobres, pero él es rico.* We're poor, but he's rich.

Usted and ustedes

Even where not strictly necessary, *usted* and *ustedes* are sometimes included and can add a degree of politeness. *¿Cómo está (usted)?* How are you? *Espero que (ustedes) vayan al cine.* I hope you are going to the movies.

Direct Object Pronouns

Just as in English, verbs can be accompanied by direct and indirect objects. A direct object is the noun or pronoun that the verb acts directly on. In a sentence such as 'I see Sam', 'Sam' is the direct object of 'see' because 'Sam' is the object that is seen. But in a sentence such as 'I am writing Sam a letter', 'Sam' is the indirect object. The item being written is 'letter', so it is the direct object. 'Sam' is the indirect object as one who is affected by the verb's action on the direct object.

If you're learning Spanish, the distinction can be important to make because Spanish, unlike English, sometimes uses different pronouns for direct and indirect objects.

Here are the direct-object pronouns along with examples of their uses:

me	me	*Juan puede ver**me**.* John can see me.
te	you singular familiar	*No **te** conoce.* He doesn't know **you**.
lo	you (singular masculine formal), him, it	*No puedo ver**lo***. I can't see **you** or I can't see **him** or I can't see **it**.
la	you (singular feminine formal), her, it	*No puedo ver**la***. I can't see **you** or I can't see **her** or I can't see **it**.
nos	us	***Nos** conocen.* They know **us**.
os	you (plural familiar)	***Os** ayudaré.* I will help you.
los	you (plural formal, masculine or mixed masculine and feminine), them (masculine or mixed masculine and feminine)	***Los** oigo.* I hear **you** or I hear **them**.
las	you (plural feminine	***Las** oigo.* I hear **you**

formal), them (feminine)	or I hear **them**.

Note : that *lo, la, los* and *las* can refer to either people or things. If they are referring to things, use the same gender as the name of the object being referred to.

Example : *Tengo dos boletos. ¿Los quieres?* (I have two tickets. Do you want them?) But, *Tengo dos rosas. ¿Las quieres?* (I have two roses. Do you want them?)

As you can see from the above examples, the location of a direct-object pronoun can vary. In most cases, it can be placed before the verb. Alternatively, it can be attached to an infinitive (the form of the verb that ends in *-ar*, *-er* or *-ir*) or a present participle (the form of the verb that ends in *-ndo*, often the equivalent of English verbs that end in '-ing'). Each sentence in the following pairs has the same meaning: *No lo puedo ver* and *no puedo verlo* (I can't see him). *Te estoy ayudando* and *estoy ayudándote* (I am helping you). Note that when the direct object is added to present participle, it is necessary to add an accent so that the stress is on the proper syllable.

Direct-object pronouns follow affirmative commands (telling someone to do something) but precede negative commands (telling someone not to do something): *estúdialo* (look at it), but *no lo estudies* (don't study it). Note again that an accent needs to be added when adding the object to the end of positive commands.

Le *as a direct object*

In some parts of Spain, *le* can substitute for *lo* as a direct object when it means 'him' but not 'it'. Less commonly in some areas, *les* can substitute for *los* when referring to people.

Indirect object Pronouns

Just as in English, verbs can be accompanied by direct and indirect objects. A direct object is the noun or pronoun that the verb acts directly on, while an indirect object is the person affected by the action but not acted directly upon. In a sentence such as 'I see Sam', 'Sam' is the direct object of 'see' because 'Sam' is the object that is seen. But in a sentence such as 'I am writing Sam a letter', 'Sam' is the indirect object. The item being written is 'letter', so 'letter' is the direct object. 'Sam' is the indirect object as one who is affected by the verb's action on the direct object.

If you're learning Spanish, the distinction can be important to make because Spanish, unlike English, sometimes uses different pronouns for direct and indirect objects.

It is also important to note that many Spanish sentences use indirect-object pronouns where a different construction is used in English. For example, ***me** pintó la casa* would typically be translated as 'he painted the house **for me**'. In fact, one sign of an indirect object in English that usually can be understood is to use 'me' as an example, as 'for me' or 'to me'. For instance, 'he bought her the ring' is the same as 'he bought the ring for her'. In that first sentence, 'her' is an indirect object. (The Spanish equivalent would be *él le compró el anillo.*)

Here are the indirect-object pronouns along with examples of their uses:

me	me	*Juan **me** da una camisa.* John is giving **me** a shirt.
te	you (singular	*Juan **te** da una camisa.* John is giving **you** a shirt.

	familiar)	
le	you (singular formal), him, her	*Juan* ***le*** *da una camisa a usted.* John is giving **you** a shirt. *Juan* ***le*** *da una camisa a él.* John is giving **him** a shirt. *Juan* ***le*** *da una camisa a ella.* John is giving **her** a shirt.
nos	us	*María* ***nos*** *da unas camisas.* Mary is giving **us** some shirts.
os	you (plural familiar)	*María* ***os*** *da unas camisas.* Mary is giving **you** some shirts.
les	you (plural formal), them	*María* ***les*** *da unas camisas.* Mary is giving **you** some shirts or Mary is giving **them** some shirts.

Note : that the direct-object and indirect-object pronouns are identical in the first and second persons. Where they differ is in the third person, where the only indirect objects (except in what is usually considered substandard speech) are *le* and *les*.

As some of the above examples indicate, an indirect-object pronoun is required whenever a sentence includes an indirect object. A further clause can be added for clarity or emphasis, but, unlike in English, an indirect pronoun is still required. For example, *le escribió* could mean 'He wrote to him', 'He wrote to her' or 'He wrote to you', depending on the context. To clarify, we can add a prepositional phrase, as in *le escribió a ella* for 'He wrote to her'. Note that *le* is still required, even though *a ella* makes it redundant.

Both direct- and indirect-object pronouns are typically placed before conjugated verbs, as in the above examples. They can be (but don't have to be) attached to infinitives and present participles: *Te voy a escribir una carta* and *voy a escribirte una carta* (I am going to write you a letter) are both correct, as are *le estoy comprando un coche* and *estoy comprándole un coche* (I am buying him a car).

In commands, direct and/or indirect objects are attached to affirmative commands but precede negative commands. *Escríbame* (write me), but *no me escribes* (don't write me).

Note : that in affirmative commands and when attaching an object to a present participle, attaching the object at the end of the verb can result in an accent being needed to keep the stress on the correct syllable.

If you have a direct object and an indirect object with the same verb, the indirect object comes first. *Te las escribo.* (I am writing them to you.)

Prepositional objects

As in English, prepositions in Spanish need an object to be completed. That object can be a noun or a pronoun (or sometimes a verb functioning as a noun).

Most of the pronouns used with prepositions in Spanish are the same as the subject pronouns, but they are different in the first- and second-person singular. Otherwise their use is fairly straightforward, as indicated in the following chart.

mí	me	*Es un regalo para **mí**.* It is a gift for **me**. *Salieron sin **mí**.*

		They left without **me**.
ti	you (singular familiar)	*Hablan de* ***ti.*** They are talking about **you**. *No valía nada mi vida antes de* ***ti.*** My life before **you** was worthless.
usted	you (singular formal)	*Las flores son para* ***usted.*** The flowers are for **you**. *Ella no tolera fumar alrededor de* ***usted.*** She doesn't put up with smoking around **you**.
él, ella	him, her	*Corrieron hacia* ***él.*** They ran toward **him**. *Fue escrito por* ***ella.*** It was written by **her**.
nosotros, nosotras	us	*Vienen tras* ***nosotros.*** They are coming after **us**. *Andan al lado de* ***nosotros.*** They are walking beside **us**.
vosotros, vosotras	you (plural familiar)	*No estoy* ***contra*** *vosotros.* I am not **against** you. *Salgo sin* ***vosotros.*** I am leaving without **you**.
ellos, ellas	them	*El coche no es* ***para*** *ellos.* The car isn't **for** them. *Salgo* ***con*** *ellas.* I am leaving **with** them.

There are two main exceptions to the above usages:

Conmigo *and* contigo

When used with *con* (usually translated as 'with') the forms *conmigo* and *contigo* are used instead of *con mí* and *con ti*, respectively.

Examples

Voy **contigo**. *¿Vas* **conmigo**? I'm going **with you**. Are you going **with me**?

Use of yo and tú with certain prepositions

The following six prepositions are used with the subject pronouns *yo* and *tú* instead of *mí* and *ti*, respectively: *entre* (usually translated as 'among' or 'between'), *excepto* ('except'), *incluso* ('including' or 'even'), *menos* ('except'), *salvo* ('except') and *según* ('according to'). Also, *hasta* is used with the subject pronouns when it is used with roughly the same meaning as *incluso*.

Examples

Es la diferencia entre **yo** *y* **tú**. It's the difference between **me** and **you** . *Muchas personas incluso/hasta* **yo** *creen en las hadas.* Many people including **me** believe in fairies or many people, even **I**, believe in fairies. *Todos excepto/ menos/salvo* **tú** *creen en las hadas.* Everybody except **you** believes in fairies. *Es la verdad según* **yo**. It's the truth according to **me**.

Demonstrative Pronouns

If you've already learned the demonstrative adjectives of Spanish, you'll find it quite easy to learn the demonstrative pronouns. They serve basically the same purpose, acting as the equivalent of 'this', 'that', 'these' or 'those' in English. The main difference is that they (like other pronouns) stand for nouns rather than modify them.

Below are the demonstrative pronouns of Spanish. Notice that they are identical to the adjectives, except that most use accent marks and that there is a neuter form (adjectives don't have a neuter form).

singular masculine	plural masculine	singular feminine	plural feminine	singular neuter
éste (this)	***éstos*** (these)	***ésta*** (this)	***éstas*** (these)	***esto*** (this)
ése (that)	***ésos*** (those)	***ésa*** (that)	***ésas*** (those)	***eso*** (that)
aquél (that)	***aquéllos*** (those)	***aquélla*** (that)	***aquéllas*** (those)	***aquello*** (that)

The accents do not affect the pronunciation, but are used merely to distinguish adjectives and pronouns. (Such accents are known as orthographic accents.) The neuter pronouns do not have accents because they have no corresponding adjective forms.

Use of the pronouns should seem straightforward, as they are used basically the same way in both English and Spanish. The key difference is Spanish requires use of the masculine pronoun when it substitutes for a masculine noun and use of the feminine pronoun when it substitutes for a feminine noun. Also, while English does use its demonstrative pronouns standing alone, it also often uses forms such as 'this one' and 'those ones'. The 'one' or 'ones' shouldn't be translated separately into Spanish.

The difference between the *ése* series of pronouns and *aquél* series is the same as the difference between the *ese* series of demonstrative adjectives and the *aquel* series. Although *ése* and *aquél* can both be translated as 'that', *aquél* is used to refer to something farther away in distance or time.

Examples

Quiero esta flor. No quiero ***ésa.*** (I want this flower. I don't want **that one**.) *Me probé muchas camisas. Voy a comprar* ***ésta.*** (I tried on many shirts. I'm going to buy **this one**.) *Me probé muchos sombreros. Voy a comprar* ***éste.*** (I tried on many hats. I'm going to buy **this one**.) *Me gustan esas casas. No me gustan* ***aquéllas.*** (I like those houses. I don't like **those over there**.)

Neuter pronouns

The neuter pronouns are never used to substitute for a specific noun. They are used to refer to an unknown object or to an idea or concept that isn't specifically named. (If you would have occasion to use a neuter plural, use the plural masculine form.) The use of *eso* is extremely common to refer to a situation that has just been stated.

Examples

¿Qué es ***esto****?* (What is **this** [unknown object]?) ***Esto*** *es bueno.* (**This** [referring to a situation rather than a specific object] is good.) *El padre de María murió. Por* ***eso****, está triste.* (Mary's father died. Because of **that**, she's sad.) *Tengo que salir a las ocho. No olvides* ***eso.*** (I have to leave at eight. Don't forget **that**.)

Possessive Pronouns

If you've already learned the long-form of the possessive adjectives, you already know the possessive pronouns of Spanish. (In fact, some grammarians classify the long-form possessive adjectives as pronouns, even though they are used to describe nouns.)

Possessive pronouns are the equivalent of the English pronouns 'mine', 'yours', 'his', 'hers', 'theirs' and 'its', but they aren't used in exactly the same way in Spanish as they are in English.

Here are the possessive pronouns of Spanish:

Pronombre	**Translation**	**Usage Examples**
mío, mía, míos, mías	mine	*Tu madre y* ***la mía*** *no pueden cantar.* (Your mother and **mine** can't sing.) *No me gustan los coches rojos.* ***El mío*** *es verde.* (I don't like red cars. **Mine** is green.)
tuyo, tuya, tuyos, tuyas	yours (singular informal)	*Este libro no es* ***mío****. Es* ***tuyo****.* (This book isn't **mine**. It's **yours**.) *¿Dónde está mi mochila?* ***La tuya*** *está aquí.* (Where is my back pack? **Yours** is here.)
suyo, suya, suyos, suyas	his, hers, yours (singular formal or plural formal), its, theirs	*Mis calcetines son rojos.* ***Los suyos*** *son negros.* (My socks are red. **His/hers/yours/theirs** are black.) *Amo a mi esposa. No ama a* ***la suya****.* (I love my wife. He doesn't love **his**.)

nuestro, nuestra, nuestros, nuestras	ours	*Este coche es* ***nuestro****.* (This car is **ours**.) *¿Te gusta tu casa? No me gusta* ***la nuestra****.* (Do you like your house? I don't like **ours**.)
vuestro, vuestra, vuestros, vuestras	yours (plural informal)	*Nuestra casa es muy vieja. ¿Y* ***la vuestra****?* (Our house is very old. And **yours**?) *No me gustan los coches de vuestros competidores. Prefiero* ***los vuestros****.* (I don't like your competitors' cars. I prefer **yours**.)

As you can see from the examples, possessive pronouns must match the noun they represent in both number and gender, just as the long-form possessive adjectives. (do)

Definite articles

Note that unlike the equivalent pronouns in English, the Spanish possessive pronouns are usually preceded by the definite article (*el, la, los* or *las*), the equivalent of 'the'. The article is usually dispensed with when the possessive pronoun follows a form of the verb *ser*, such as *son* or *es*, as in the examples, although it is sometimes retained for emphasis.

Ambiguous suyo

Suyo and the related forms can be ambiguous, since they can mean 'his', 'hers', 'yours', 'theirs' or 'its'. When context doesn't make its meaning clear, the possessive pronoun can be omitted and replaced by a prepositional phrase such as *de él* (instead of 'his') or *de ellos* (instead of 'theirs'). **Examples:** *No es mi coche. Es de ella.* (It's not my car. It's hers.) *¿Dónde están mis zapatos? Los de él están aquí.* (Where are my shoes? His are here.)

The single, masculine form of the pronouns can also be treated as neuter and thus be preceded by the neuter definite article *lo*. Even though singular, the pronoun can stand for more than one object. The neuter form is used when no specific object is being referred to.

Examples

No toques lo mío. (Don't touch what is mine. Don't touch my things.) *Lo mío es importante.* (What is mine is important. My things are important.)

Interrogative Pronouns

As their name suggests, interrogative pronouns are those pronouns that are used almost exclusively in questions. As in English, interrogative pronouns are typically placed at or very near the beginning of a sentence.

Following are the interrogative pronouns in Spanish with examples of their usage. Note that in some cases the pronouns can vary in translation when they follow a preposition. Also, some of the pronouns existing in singular and plural forms and in the case of *cuánto* masculine and feminine forms should match the noun they stand for.

Pronoun	**Translation**	**Examples**
quién, quiénes	who, whom	*¿Quién es tu amiga?* (Who is your friend?)

		¿Quién es? (Who is it?) *¿A quiénes conociste?* (Whom have you met?) *¿Con quién andas?* (Whom are you walking with?) *¿De quién es esta computadora?* (Whose computer is this?) *¿Para quiénes son las comidas?* (Whom are the meals for?)
qué	what (The phrases *por qué* and *para qué* are usually translated as 'why'. *Por qué* is more common than *para qué*. They are sometimes	*¿Qué es esto?* (What is this?) *¿Qué pasa?* (What's happening?) *¿En qué piensas?* (What are you thinking about?) *¿De que hablas?* (What are you talking about?)
	interchangeable; *para qué* can be used only when asking about the intent or purpose of something	*¿Para qué estudiaba español?* (Why did you study Spanish? What did you study Spanish for?) *¿Por*

	happening and can be thought of as meaning 'what for'.)	*qué se averió el coche?* (Why did the car break down?)
dónde	where (to say 'to where' use *adónde* instead of *a dónde*, which usually is considered old-fashioned)	*¿Dónde está?* (Where is it?) *¿De dónde es Roberto?* (Where is Roberto from?) *¿Adónde vas?* (Where are you going to?)
cuándo	when	*¿Cuándo salimos?* (When are we leaving?) *¿Para cuándo estará listo?* (For when will it be ready?) *¿Hasta cuándo quedan ustedes?* (Until when are you staying?)
cuál, cuáles	which one, which ones (This word also can often be translated as 'what'. Generally speaking, when *cuál* is used it suggests the making of a selection from more than one alternative.)	*¿Cuál prefieres?* (Which one do you prefer?) *¿Cuáles prefieres?* (Which ones do you prefer?)

cómo	how	*¿Cómo estás?* (How are you?) *¿Cómo lo haces?* (How do you do it?)
cuánto, cuánta, cuántos, cuántas	how much, how many	*¿Cuánto hay?* (How much is there?) *¿Cuántos?* (How many?) [The masculine form is used unless in context it is known you are referring to an object or objects that are grammatically feminine. For example, *¿cuántos?* might mean 'how many pesos?' because peso is masculine, while *¿cuántas?* might mean 'how many towels?' because *toalla* is feminine.]

As you may have noticed, the interrogative pronouns are all spelled with accent marks that do not affect the pronunciation. Many of the interrogative pronouns also can be used in statements (as opposed to questions) without the accent marks. Note also that many of the interrogative pronouns can be used as other parts of speech, including adjectives and adverbs, either with or without the accent marks.)

Indefinite Pronouns

Indefinite pronouns are those pronouns that typically refer to no particular person or thing. The chart below indicates which pronouns these are in both English and Spanish.

In Spanish as in English, most of the words used as indefinite pronouns sometimes function as other parts of speech, often as adjectives and sometimes as adverbs. In Spanish, some of the indefinite pronouns exist in both masculine and feminine forms as well as singular and plural forms, so they must agree with the nouns they refer to.

Here are the indefinite pronouns of Spanish:

Pronoun	**Translation**	**Examples**
alguien	someone, somebody, anyone, anybody	*Necesito a* ***alguien*** *que pueda escribir.* (I need **someone** who can write.) *¿Me llamó* ***alguien?*** (Did **anybody** call me?)
algo	something	*Veo* ***algo*** *grande y blanco.* (I see **something** big and white.) *¿Aprendiste* ***algo*** *esta tarde?* (Did

		you learn **something** this afternoon?)
alguno, alguna, algunos, algunas	one, some (things or people)	*Puedes suscribirte a **alguno** de nuestros servicios.* (You can subscribe to **one** of our services.) *¿Quieres **alguno** más?* (Do you want **some** more?) *Voy a estudiar con **algunas** de las madres.* (I'm going to study with some of the mothers.) ***Algunos** quieren salir.* (Some want to leave.)
cualquiera	anybody, *anyone*	***Cualquiera** puede tocar la guitarra.* (**Anyone** can play the guitar.)

Notes : The plural form, *cualesquiera*, is seldom used.

mucho, mucha, muchos, muchas	much, many	*Me queda **mucho** por hacer.* (I have **much** left to do.) *La escuela tiene **mucho** que*

		ofrecer. (The school has **much** to offer.) *Somos* ***muchos.*** (There are **many** of us. *Literally,* we are **many**.)
nada	nothing	***Nada*** *parece cierto.* (Nothing seems certain.) *No tengo* ***nada.*** (I have nothing.)

Notes : When *nada* follows a verb, the part of the sentence preceding the verb typically is also put in negative form.

nadie	nobody, no one	***Nadie*** *me cree.* (Nobody believes me.) *No conozco a* ***nadie.*** (I know **nobody**.)

Notes : When *nadie* follows a verb, the part of the sentence preceding the verb typically is also put in negative form.

ninguno, ninguna	none, nobody, no one	***Ninguna*** *de ellas va al parque.* (**None** of them are going to the park.) *No conozco a* ***ninguno.*** (I know **nobody**.)
otro, otra, otros, otras	another, other one, another one,	*Quiero* ***otro.*** (I want **another one**.) *Los* ***otros***

	other ones, others	*van al parque.* (The **others** are going to the park.)
poco, pocos, pocas	little, little bit, few, a few	*Tengo un **poco** de miedo.* (I have a **little bit** of fear.) ***Pocos** van al parque.* (**A few** are going to the park.)
todo, todos, todas	everything, all, everyone	*Él comió **(todo)**.* (He ate **everything**.) ***Todos** van al parque.* (**All** are going to the park.)
uno, una, unos, unas	one, some	***Uno** no puede creer sin hacer.* (**One** cannot believe without doing.) ***Unos** quieren ganar más.* (**Some** want to earn more.) *Comí **uno** y deseché el otro.* (I ate **one** and threw away the other.)

Although some different pronouns are translated the same into English, they aren't necessarily interchangeable. Explaining some of the subtle differences in usage is beyond the scope of this Chapter. In many cases, the pronouns can be translated in more than one way into English; you must rely on context in those cases to convey the meaning.

Que And Other Relative Pronouns

Relative pronouns can be used quite differently in Spanish than in English and the fine points of their use goes well beyond what would be expected of beginners. So keep in mind that most of this Chapter focuses on the most common usages; as you learn Spanish you will learn other sentence constructions as well.

Relative pronouns are pronouns that are used to introduce a clause that provides more information about a noun. Thus in the sentence 'The man who is singing is my father', the relative pronoun is 'who'; the clause 'who is singing' provides further information about the sentence's subject, 'the man'. In the Spanish equivalent, *el hombre que canta es mi padre*, the relative pronoun is *que*.

Common relative pronouns in English include 'that', 'which', 'who', 'whom' and 'whose' (although these words also have other uses). In Spanish, by far the most common relative pronoun is *que*. As can be seen in the following sentences, it usually means 'that', 'which' or 'who'.

Espero ***que*** *venga.* (I hope **that** he comes.)

Tiene los zapatos ***que*** *necesita.* (She has the shoes **that** she needs.)

Conozco a los niños ***que*** *estaban aquí.* (I know the boys **who** were here.)

Compré el coche en ***que*** *íbamos.* (I bought the car in **which** we rode.)

Mi hermano es el hombre ***que*** *salió.* (My brother is the man **who** left.)

Omission of 'that' in English

Note that in the first two sentences above, the word 'that' can be omitted in English. However, in Spanish the relative pronoun **cannot** be omitted. Notice how the following examples use a relative pronoun that isn't included in the first English translation:

Es cierto ***que*** *él va a ganar.* (It is certain he is going to win. It is certain **that** he is going to win.)

¿Dónde está el periódico ***que*** *compré esta mañana?* (Where is the newspaper I bought this morning? Where is the newspaper **that** I bought this morning?)

Ella me dijo ***que*** *va al cine.* (She told me she is going to the movies. She told me **that** she is going to the movies.)

Other relative pronouns

As a beginner, you likely won't need to use the other relative pronouns of Spanish, but you certainly will come across them in writing and speech. At this point, you don't need to learn the rules of their usage, but you should recognise them when you see or hear them. Here they are with examples of their usage:

Pronoun	**Common translations**	**Examples**
quien, quienes	who, whom	*Es el médico de* ***quien*** *le dije.* (He is the doctor **whom** I told you about.) *Conozco a Sofía,* ***quien*** *tiene dos coches.* (I know Sophia, who has two cars.)
el cual, la cual, lo cual, los cuales, las cuales	which, who, whom	*Rebeca es la mujer con* ***la cual*** *vas a viajar.* (Rebeca is the woman with **whom** you are going to travel.)

el que, la que, lo que, los que, las que	which, who, whom	*Rebeca es la mujer con* ***la que*** *vas a viajar.* (Rebeca is the woman with **whom** you are going to travel.)
cuyo, cuya, cuyos, cuyas	whose	*Es la profesora* ***cuyo*** *hijo tiene el coche.* (She is the teacher **whose** son has the car.)
donde	where	*Voy al mercado* ***donde*** *se venden manzanas.* (I'm going to the market **where** they sell apples.)

Reflexive Pronouns

Rcflcxivc pronouns are used in both Spanish and English whenever the subject of a verb is also its object. In other words, reflexive pronouns are used when the subject of a sentence is acting on itself. An example is the *me* in *me veo* (and the corresponding 'myself' in 'I see myself'), where the person seeing and the person seen are the same.

Verbs used with a reflexive pronoun are known either as reflexive verbs or pronominal verbs.

Reflexive pronouns are used in much the same way as direct-object and indirect-object pronouns; they typically precede the verb or are attached to the infinitive. In fact, reflexive pronouns are identical with the other object pronouns except in the third person and second-person (informal and plural). Here are the reflexive pronouns:

Pronoun	Translation	Examples
me	myself	*Me lavo.* (I am washing myself.) *Voy a elegir**me**.* (I am going to choose **myself**.)
te	yourself (informal)	*¿**Te** odias?* (Do you hate **yourself**?) *¿Puedes ver**te**?* (Can you see yourself?)
se	himself, herself, itself, themselves, yourself (formal), yourselves (formal), each other	*Roberto **se** adora.* (Roberto adores **himself**.) *La niña prefiere vestir**se**.* (The girl prefers to dress **herself**.) *La historia **se** repite.* (History repeats **itself**.) ***Se** compran los regalos.* (They are buying **themselves** gifts or they are buying **each other** gifts.) *¿Se afeita Ud.?* (Do you shave yourself?)
nos	ourselves, each other	***Nos** respetamos.* (*We respect **ourselves** or we*

		respect ***each other***.) *No podemos ver****nos***. (*We can't see* ***each other*** *or we can't see* ***ourselves***.)
os	yourselves (informal), each other	*Es evidente que* ***os*** *queréis. (It's obvious that you love* ***each other*** *or it's obvious you love* ***yourselves***.) Podéis ayudar**os**. (*You can help* ***yourselves*** *or you can help* ***each other***.)

Learning to use reflexive pronouns, especially *se* in Spanish, can be challenging, since they are used more frequently and for additional purposes in Spanish. This Chapter, therefore, is an introduction only to those cases where reflexive pronouns are used similarly in the two languages. As you study Spanish, you will frequently come across sentences where reflexive pronouns are used but where they may not readily be translated to English reflexive pronouns.

As you can see from the above examples, the plural pronouns in Spanish can be translated using the English reflexive pronouns or the phrase 'each other'. (*Technically, grammarians would call such a usage of the Spanish pronoun reciprocal rather than reflexive.*) Usually, context will make clear the most likely translation. Thus, while *nos escribimos* conceivably could mean 'we write to ourselves', it most often would mean 'we write to each other'. If necessary, a phrase can be added for clarification, such as in *se golpean el uno a otro* (*they are hitting each other*) and *se golpean a sí mismos* (*they are hitting themselves*).

Reflexive pronouns should not be confused with English constructions such as 'I myself am buying the gift'. In that sentence (which could be translated to Spanish as *yo mismo compro el regalo*), 'myself' isn't being used as a reflexive pronoun but as a way of adding emphasis.

Introducing Se

Se is undoubtedly the most versatile of the Spanish pronouns. As you learn Spanish, you will come across *se* used in a variety of ways. For the beginner, it isn't necessary to learn all those ways, although it can be helpful to be introduced to its various uses to help avoid confusion when you see it used in a way you haven't studied yet.

Here are the major uses of *se*, along with examples in sentences:

As a reflexive pronoun

This is its most common use. As is explained in the Chapter on reflexive pronouns, such pronouns indicate that the subject of a verb is also its object. In English, this is usually accomplished by using pronouns such as 'himself' or 'themselves'. *Se* is used as the reflexive pronoun for third-person uses (*including when usted or ustedes is the subject*). Some verbs (*as in the final two examples below*) can be used reflexively in Spanish even though they aren't translated that way in English.

Examples

Pablo ***se*** *ve por el espejo.* (*Pablo sees* ***himself*** *using the mirror.*) *Los padres no pueden oír****se****.* (*The parents can't hear* ***themselves****.*) *Rebecca se perjudica por fumar.* (*Rebecca is hurting* ***herself*** *by smoking.*) *Benjamín Franklin* ***se levantaba*** *temprano.* (*Benjamin Franklin* ***got up*** *early.*) ***Se comió*** *los tacos.* (*He* ***ate up*** *the snacks.*)

As the equivalent of the English passive voice

By using *se*, particularly when discussing inanimate objects, it is possible to indicate some sort of action without indicating who performed the action. Grammatically, such sentences are structured in the same way that sentences using reflexive verbs are. Thus in a literal sense, a sentence such as *se venden coches* means. 'cars sell themselves'. In actuality, however, such a sentence would be the English equivalent of 'cars are sold' or, more loosely translated, 'cars for sale'.

Examples: ***Se abren*** *las puertas.* (*The doors are opened.*) ***Se vendió*** *la computadora.* (*The computer* ***was sold****.*) ***(Se perdieron)*** *(las llaves).* (*The keys* ***were lost****.*) ***Se prohibe*** *fumar.* (*Smoking* ***is prohibited****.*)

***As a substitute for* le *or* les**

When the indirect-object pronoun *le* or *les* is immediately followed by another pronoun that begins with an *l*, the *le* or *les* is changed to *se*, apparently as a way to avoid having two pronouns in a row beginning with the *l* sound.

Examples

*Dé**se**lo a ella.* (*Give it* ***to her***.) **Se** lo dijo a él. (*He told it* ***to him***.) *No* ***se*** *lo voy a dar a ellos.* (*I'm not going to give it* ***to them***.)

The impersonal se

In some sentences, *se* is used in an impersonal sense with singular verbs to indicate that people in general or no person in particular, performs the action. As the examples below show, there are variety of ways such sentences can be translated to English.

Examples

Se maneja *rápidamente en Lima.* (***People drive*** *fast in Lima.*) ***Se puede*** *encontrar cocos en el mercado.* (***You can*** *find coconuts in the market.*) *Muchas veces* ***se tiene que*** *estudiar para aprender.* (*Often* ***you have to*** *study to learn.*) ***No se debe*** *comer de prisa.* (***One ought not*** *to eat quickly.*)

Lesson 11

Greetings in Spanish

First impressions count. That's one reason you should learn some of these common greetings before visiting an area where Spanish is spoken. Even if your knowledge of Spanish is rudimentary, it can make your conversation a bit smoother to know some of these statements or questions of common courtesy.

Phrases in common use can vary with location and sometimes with age or social status. But except where indicated, those listed on the page can be used appropriately in almost any situation.

Hola

Hello, hi

Hola, aló, jaló, bueno, al, diga

Hello *(on the telephone)*

The choice of telephone greeting varies with location.

Adiós

Goodbye

An informal alternative in some areas is **chau** *(sometimes spelled ciao, from Italian).*

¿Cómo estás? ¿Cómo está?

How are you?

Muy bien, gracias

Very well, thank you

Buenos días

Good day, good morning

In some areas, a shortened form, *buen día*, is used.

Buenas tardes

Good afternoon

Buenas tardes also should be used in the early evening in preference to *buenas noches.*

Buenas noches

Good night

Buenas noches can be used as a greeting as well as a farewell.

¿Cómo te va? ¿Cómo le va?1 ¿Qué tal? ¿Qué hay?

How's it going? What's happening?

¿Qué pasa?

What's happening?

¿Qué hubo? ¿Qué onda?

How is it going? What's happening?

These phrases are most common in Mexico.

¿Cómo te llamas? ¿Cómo se llama usted?[2]

What's your name?

A literal translation would be 'What do you call yourself?' or, somewhat less literally, 'What are you called?'

Me llamo Chris.

My name is Chris.

A literal translation would be 'I call myself Chris' or, somewhat less literally, 'I am called Chris'.

Mucho gusto. Encantado.

It's a pleasure to meet you.

These literally mean 'much pleasure' and 'delighted', respectively, so they would have different meanings in other contexts.

Bienvenido, bienvenida, bienvenidos, bienvenidas

Welcome

Lesson 12

Asking for Directions

There are few things more frustrating while travelling than getting lost. Fortunately, if you're travelling in an area where Spanish is spoken, this list of phrases and words can be of help. Combine the vocabulary listed here with basic grammar found in the accompanying Chapters and you'll be well on your way to getting the help you need. Even if you're not proficient in Spanish, in most places you travel you'll find that people will appreciate your desire to use their language. *¡Buen viaje! (Have a great trip!)*

¿Dónde está … ? ¿Dónde están … ?

Where is … ? Where are … ?

¿Por dónde se va a … ? Or, ¿Cómo puedo llegar a … ?

How do you go to … ?

¿Dónde estamos aquí en el mapa?

Where are we on the map?

¿Está lejos? ¿Está por aquí?

Is it far away? Is it near here?

Busco ...

I'm looking for ...

Estoy perdido (perdida if you're female).

I'm lost.

Latin America: ¿Dónde puedo tomar un taxi (un autobús)? Spain: ¿Dónde puedo coger un taxi (un autobús)? (Notes: Other terms used regionally for 'bus' include bus, colectivo, camión, camioneta, góndola, guagua, micro, microbús and pullman. Be careful with usage of the verb coger in parts of Latin America, because it can have an obscene meaning.)

Where can I catch a taxi *(a bus)*?

Escríbalo, por favor.

Write it down, please.

Hágame el favor de hablar más despacio.

Speak more slowly, please.

No entiendo bien el español.

I don't understand Spanish well.

¿Hay alguien que habla inglés?

Is there anyone who speaks English?

norte, este or oriente, oeste or occidente, sur

north, east, west, south

kilómetro, milla, metro

kilometre, mile, metre

calle, avenida, camino or carretera

street, avenue, highway

cuadra (Latin America) or manzana (Spain)

city block

esquina

street corner

dirección

address

Lesson 13

Counting in Spanish

Although Spanish numbers can be memorised in a straightforward way, their use can be confusing for persons new to Spanish. Numbers made up of more than one part are often formed differently than they are in English and some Spanish numbers change according to the gender of the nouns they apply to.

Following are the basic Spanish numbers and patterns in which they are formed. Those that are in italics are forms that change according to gender, while the non-italic forms are fixed.

1	*uno*
2	dos
3	tres
4	cuatro
5	cinco
6	seis
7	siete
8	ocho
9	nueve
10	diez

11	once
12	doce
13	trece
14	catorce
15	quince
16	dieciséis
17	diecisiete
18	dieciocho
19	diecinueve
20	veinte
21	*veintiuno*
22	veintidós
23	veintitrés
24	veinticuatro
25	veinticinco
26	veintiséis
27	veintisiete
28	veintiocho
29	veintinueve
30	treinta
31	*treinta y uno*
32	treinta y dos
33	treinta y tres
40	cuarenta
41	*cuarenta y uno*
42	cuarenta y dos
50	cincuenta
60	sesenta
70	setenta
80	ochenta
90	noventa
100	ciento, cien
101	*ciento uno*
102	ciento dos

103	ciento tres
110	ciento diez
199	ciento noventa y nueve
200	*doscientos*
201	*doscientos uno*
202	*doscientos dos*
203	*doscientos tres*
251	*doscientos cincuenta y uno*
252	doscientos cincuenta y dos
300	*trescientos*
400	*cuatrocientos*
500	*quinientos*
600	*seiscientos*
700	*setecientos*
800	*ochocientos*
900	*novecientos*
1.000	mil
2.000	dos mil
3.000	tres mil
3.333	*tres mil trescientos treinta y* tres
1,000,000	un millón
1,000,000,000	mil millones

Shortening uno *and* ciento

Uno and numbers ending in *-uno* are shortened to *un* when they immediately precede a masculine noun. When standing alone *(that is, being 100 exactly) ciento* is shortened to *cien* before preceding a noun of either gender; the longer form is used within longer numbers (*except when preceding mil)*.

Examples

un lápiz (1 pencil), una pluma (1 pen), cincuenta y un

lápices (51 pencils), cincuenta y una plumas (51 pens), cien lápices (100 pencils), cien plumas (100 pens), ciento tres lápices (103 pencils), *ciento tres plumas (103 pens), cien mil lápices (100,000 pencils), cien mil plumas (100,000 pens)*

Gender

As indicated above, the italicised portions of numbers vary according to gender. When a number ends in *-uno* ('one'), the form *-un* is used before masculine nouns and -*una* before feminine nouns. The *uno* form is used only in counting. Accent marks are used where needed to maintain the correct pronunciation. The hundreds portions of numbers change in gender even when other parts of the number intervene before the noun.

Examples

un coche (1 car), una casa (1 house), veintiún coches (21 cars), veintiuna casas (21 houses), doscientos coches (200 cars), doscientas casas (200 houses), doscientos dos coches (202 cars), doscientas dos casas (202 houses).

Punctuation

In most of the Spanish-speaking world, periods and commas within numbers are reversed from what they are in U.S. English. Thus in Spain *1.234,567* would be the way of writing *mil doscientos treinta y cuatro coma quinientos sesenta y siete* or what would be written in the United States as 1,234.567. In Mexico, Central America and Puerto Rico, numbers usually are punctuated as they are in the United States.

Lesson 14

Telling Time

If you can count to 29 in Spanish, you can tell time. The basic way of telling time in Spanish is to use the singular form of *ser ('to be')*, which is *es*, for one o'clock and the plural form, *son*, for other times. Minutes can be stated simply by separating them from the hour using *y*, the word for 'and'.

Es la una

It is 1:00.

Es la una y dos.

It is 1:02.

Son las dos.

It is 2:00.

Son las tres.

It is 3:00.

Son las seis y cinco.

It is 6:05.

Son las siete y diez.

It is 7:10.

Son las once y diecinueve.

It is 11:19.

To indicate the half hour, use *media*. Use *cuarto* to indicate the quarter hours.

Es la una y media.

It is 1:30.

Son las cuatro y media.

It is 4:30.

Es la una y cuarto.

It is 1:15.

It is customary to use *menos* to tell time during the second half of each hour, stating the number of minutes until the following hour.

Es la una menos diez.

It is 12:50. (It is ten until one.)

Son las cinco menos cinco.

It is 4:55. (It is five until five.)

Son las diez menos veinte.

It is 9:40. (It is twenty until ten.)

Son las ocho menos cuarto.

It is 7:45. *(It is quarter until eight.)*

In most of the Spanish-speaking world, both 12-hour and 24-hour clocks are used, the latter being quite common in schedules and similar printed materials. To indicate time of day when using the 12-hour clock, use *de la mañana* before noon (*mediodía*), *de la tarde* between noon and early evening and *de la noche* between then and midnight (*medianoche*).

Es medianoche.

It's midnight.

Son las siete y cuarto de la mañana.

It's 7:15 a.m. *(It is 7:15 in the morning.)*

Es mediodía.

It's noon.

Son las cuarto menos cinco de la tarde.

It's 3:55 p.m. *(It is five before four in the afternoon.)*

Son las ocho y media de la noche.

It's 8:30 p.m. *(It is eight and a half at night.)*

Here are some other time-related expressions that can be useful:

Son las tres y cuarto en punto.

It's 3:15 exactly.

Son las seis y media más o menos.

It's about 6:30.

Salimos a las nueve.

We are leaving at 9:00.

***Era** la una. **Eran** los dos (tres, cuatro, etc.).*

It was 1:00. It was 2:00 (3:00, 4:00, etc.).

Buenos días.

Good day, good morning.

Buenas tardes.

Good afternoon, good evening (until about 8 p.m.).

Buenas noches.

Good evening, good night (as either a greeting or a farewell).

¿Qué hora es?

What time is it?

¿Cuándo ...?

When ... ?